Broken Fist

Recollection from the Tombs of Time

AJIT SINGH

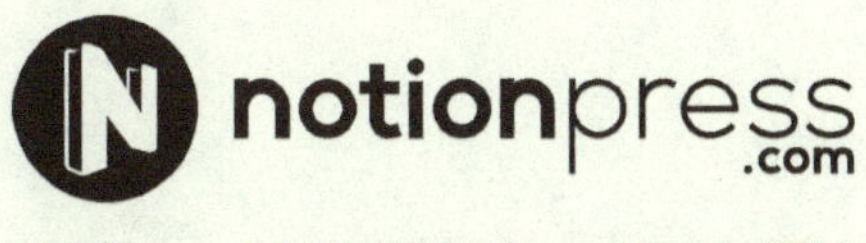

INDIA • SINGAPORE • MALAYSIA

ISBN

Paperback: 979-8-89277-994-4

Hardcase: 979-8-89322-921-9

Contents

PART 2

Preface

Broken Fist is a collection of short poems based on pages of the past, with its primary objective being to show the stages of evolution through which mankind has passed. Conceived in 2015 with the advent of social media platforms, Broken Fist initially embarked on a love sojourn.

However, its nomenclature changed, transforming it into a journey from the past present and finally into the future. This collection of 150 poems depicts the stages of human progress, traveling from the stone age to the metal age, from the birth of gigantic civilizations that ruled with the might of the sword to their mightiest fall. It explores the coming of the industrial revolution and the birth of its brainchild, capitalism.

The greatest invention of the human mind was the discovery of agriculture. It was the reason for bringing collective associations into the lives of people. For the first time, people started living as social groups. Tribes came into existence, and with them, tribal chiefs wielded considerable authority. The dominant role played by the authority in framing regulations for running the affairs of tribes was the first taste of unlimited power wielded by the authority. The early man, lost in jungles, discovered the magic of power to control the lives of others, and with it started the scramble for power within the tribes. The follies of the human mind exposed, as collective living succeeded in driving a wedge among the traditional tribal living.

War is in the minds of humans, and this proved true to its last word. Enormous civilizations such as Greek, Persian, and Roman based their influence on military prowess. They kept on grappling for centuries, destroying each other in the process. No one was the winner, but everybody was a loser.

The fragility of the human mind was the way in for ever-parching peace spreaders to preach the gospel of truth, reason, and benevolence.

Pious religion-seeking humanity, suffering from the ravages of war, were overwhelmed by the scale of cruelty meted out to humanity. Religions such as Christianity, Buddhism, which preached non-violence emerged from the wails of those times. People flocked to these preachers thinking that they would provide the much needed relief from the cruel tyrants. Men of peace were often looked with disdain by the ones who believed in violent methods to overcome in what they believed was a loomimg threat on their fiefdoms.

Broken fist is an attempt to bring to contemporary living the aspects of two opposing forces of present day existence which work at cross purposes. The ones against any change of methods and processes and the one always seeking change for better.

The dominant forces have been able to form coherent social groups with active political support to stop any modern thought from interfering in day today affairs of the people. Any aspect of minute changes advocated by democratic thought are meant to be stopped or even thwarted at any cost. This has been a rule rather than a norm of living since people started living in societies. Many of the reflections in this collection of poems makes extensive use of events which have influenced the world in many ways. To say something events in verses has never been experimented in the past.

This humble attempt seeks to present the events on which volumes of literature have been attempted in the past. The short sketches of poetic verses have a deep meaning assigned to them than just a stream of thoughts strung together by words.

The existence of the universe leaving aside the scientific principles governing the laws of the cosmic world would still be determined by the blood thirsty tyrants of the past or even hate filled humans in form of powerful dictators of the present. It needs to be remembered that tyrants of the past had the legitimacy of the sword to force their will upon the masses of humanity and the dictators who never left a stone unturned to bring the world to brink of disaster acquire the nod of modern democratic methods to rule. Both the forms challenge the basic norms of cooperative co existence. The sum and substance of this collection has Peace as its central focus. The oldest religious text of the cosmic universe i.e. the VEDAS have explicitly mentioned about the state of equilibrium which the world looks up to after destruction and chaos witnessed by ways of wars and holocausts.

In one of the sayings contained in the VEDAS which has said that let noble thoughts come from everywhere, or even the one stating that world is a bond of brotherhood were thought about millions of years ago by Indian sages. In true sense these thoughts were the forerunners of the economic phenomena of global village which ultimately led to the economic revival of the world by creation of multinational business companies. The central thread running through the times is the craving of peace since no visible progression would take place unless efforts are afoot to make peace happen. It would be difficult to imagine flourishing of economic units with all the bombs and modern day amputations taking place around. Such is the resounding impact of peace initiatives throughout the world.

BROKEN FIST is not a chronological version on happenings taking place in the world. Its spontaneous in nature and at times volatile in presentation. It brings on board on how the sword overcame the mind of reason, on how power crushed anything which was sane and perfectly in tune with the changing times. It takes exclusive footage from events which keep on happening from time to time impacting lives of people. It's not a paste and copy affair but verses which come from original mind looking at the past and how the future could be improved.

Broken fist is not a big intellectual leap of exploring the past and discovering the present or looking into future its simple objective is to make the art of poetry strike roots in minds of readers for everlasting joy and introspection.

Ajit Jamwal

21 January 2024

Conquerors have been ordained, worshipped, made to worship like deities for whatever they inflicted on the world. This piece of prose written on 3rd of March 2016 was titled as the fright of gallows. Ordinary men and women just want to eke out a living leaving aside what is happening around them. The palpable fear of death, leaving alone whom they cared for makes them harried rabbits searching for a burrow to bide time.

The Fright of The Gallows

Heroes all
Not the shining armor
or the knights galloping to glory plain people with wide open eyes

The disrobe of mother earth
Not one of those to watch with acclaim countless faces facing wrath of aliens

Smoking guns silenced death roll rattles
A few graves, or woods decked on heaps, Armies of no consequence
no fire to repel
ripped souls, shredded ambitions

A century to the fore sunshine of freedom bathes kingdom of slaves
yoke of aliens a never ending burden

Of our own stock
dark hearts with engulfed minds
barter the land for self bestowed gifts rebirth of alien monsters
price out the purses no heroes in view
cheer leaders join the chorus

Piracy of ages, blood in cool freeze rabbits scared by precussions thrones of calcium sticks
A spectacle from the monotonous sights crushed by desires of motives
some heroes to be worshipped of different stature.

Wars have always excited humans of dominant virtues. They have been happening on the face of the earth since the time of some soul coming up with the idea of big bang theory. They occur and continue to occur despite the shout from some peace brigade calling for their immediate stop but to no avail. It's almost on finger tips now. A innocent child is mind washed about the century old war called the crusades. He or she grows up in a stifling atmosphere of fear and mistrust. As if to bolster his already stacked mind the very idea of two universal wars comes up to him. And the volcano of consistent battle literature is fed into his innocent self till the time his mind is made up to wreck something which was beyond a comprehend of an innocent mind.

What's Left Out of War

What's left out of war

some ruins, lonely patches of blood
Birds of prey hanging over stretches
What's left of a war

Ego minced and prides silenced a thousand enemies and non to friendly

no prosperity just a satisfied blood lust what's left of a war

Humanity disgraced, a civilization termed abusive Those whom we thought belonging to a fraternity became cutthroat savaged to madness
what's left of a war

Might of human minds in ruins toil of decades in trash
to remind when they occurred
a journey through a valley of lost hope what's left of a war

Some recollections of cities blinded in dry gun powder everything within the arc amess of mangled mass destruction supreme, devastation heaped
this happened a century ago

still no lessons learned, no morals gained still on path of assured slaughter
what's left of a war

Orphans, widows, toddlers in cradles elderly walking with support sticks since the able bodied were made to sleep in the guise of nationalistic spirits screaming cries of patriotic fervor what's left of a war

An account of indelible imprint
of and by humans perceived as tyrants
of armies led into battlefields blindfolded what's left of a war

Humanity has no believers, very often it is taken as a dying emotion better to be ignored. It's a controversy of sorts when people kneel down to those who have preached the virtues of humanity. It's not piting the ones who are less fortunate to be born with frugal means. There have been instances from the volumes of history before where class struggle has been the cause of upheavals witnessed. The crusade of colonies to uproot an empire where the sun would never set. Largely greed of what's can be called the white race was sole cause of disturbances seen in 18th and 19th century. Times were to be seen which were the bloodiest since the inception of the blue planet.

A Marooned Fate

Shipwrecked and in deep quicksand a marooned humanity
of a century of conflicts, borne from the minds
They have to have reconciled by now In utter disregard its now known

Guns and daggers drawn at each other nations go hammer and tongs at each other
throughout the forgotten chronicles of history the wisest say, its all gone with the clock

look forward for a rainbow in the overgrown mist

clouding the mind with dark vibes a pessimist gets nowhere
time tells a blood curling tale

Settlements turned to heaps of concrete rubble beneath lie in
thousands half dead bodies Sirens, screams, air raids
Tanks, guns filled with arsenal of deadly kind

Scurrying pack of hares
not a hole in sight for escape no army to defend poor souls
spectacle watched by the mighty

Sickly armed, cultivated bondage, an antic of piece called human suffering
No written testament of fortune digger to hold

Made to track the oath of nationalism follow code of faith ethics
Traitors shout the scoundrels Kill him, hang him, bury him
Hang his carcass by preserving with spices

Long ago in city of sword might
a tale written by a ragged vagabond there lived a rebel in every breath
some to be gallowed, others, to be swallowed while some to be followed

Revolutionaries have a deep impact on the thinking of the masses. Many of them continue to exist in hearts of countrymen till now. All of them continue to inspire people to believe in nationalistic sentiment without expecting Anything in return. This selfless thought and unwavering love for the country distiguishes them from the rest of the people. They may have be silenced by the forces which believed in subjugation of the popular will. Even now the most well known and famous people living in any nation of the world are the soldiers of the country. They keep on fighting for their countrymen in deserts, mountains, jungles, and even in marshes. This poem recalls the way in which these revolutionaries keep their spirits alive amid the punishments bestowed on them by kings, tyrants, dictators, and the colonizers.

Gallows,Gallows,Gallows

The deafening crescendo descended upon the vampire seats
Somewhere from somewhere the bullets struck
in the eye of the heart failed to bleed it dry
The last minutes of journey called life

Thieves, robbers, scoundrels, lost in charm dreams Hoarders fall upon a pile of helpless
plough wielding saints, feeding and watering they kill, mow, and sow seeds of hatred
Chained in their own cages times watch the spectacle

Centuries roll by, slaves of destiny
In need of a messiah, even the gods turned their backs Then from almost an alien event
A soul lived to replenish the dead with vigor coffins

No great man with loads of gifted treasures
He infused the spirits of half dead lying in still In short span he wrote a glittering spellbind
As the noose settled around his neck
Some last words for dear countrymen he loved

Crusades or 100 years between Christians and Muslims was the most lengthy war fought solely for gaining religious supremacy. The later wars were due to scramble for colonies and the Greed to exploit the economic resources of the colonies. Crusades or most aptly religious wars were mostly spurned by religious bigots blinded by faith and charged with the ambition of spreading religion by force. The bi polar religious bent of the western world in medieval times was as a result of backwardness in education advancement. It was only when Renaissance and reformation arrived in Europe that the frequency of religious wars decreased. The wars mostly fought for revival of holy lands as the Christians called them from the Muslims. The cry of religion united the Christians like never before.

A Fruitless Endeavor

Lost the count for the length of decades it was fought
Armies collected by a religion cry
Wars of no significance as giant religious machineries clashed
Washing away the pious rights of religions to bring in some sooth to mankind
Beleaguered the civilizations that gave sanction to them
Configurations worked out by the popes and ulama
Of the holy cross or the pious Masjid
Millions perished on those cruel battlefields in name of a faith
A death of scriptures an insult to the relics
Earth of green crops and exciting flora
A sight of never ending mortuary spread in corners
Of what use these holy wars
Sentiments softer than heart beats
A zeal called religion or blinding agony of hate and deceive
For when killing in its name is all against cannons of living
Surrender thy self before self possessed hate
The preachers in their wildest dreams
Spoke in length about the ways of living
All forgotten in flash of a sacrilegious thunder
A wonder of wonders the religious hatred becomes a meek surrender

India was a land of large evil social customs which prevailed in a male dominated society. With no means of advanced education these customs were practiced mostly with force. Father of Indian nationalism, Raja Ram Mohan Roy was the first major public figure to speak openly against various cruel customs like Sati, child marriage, women education and widow remarriage. In his efforts to undo the society of these inhuman and barbaric practices he was ably supported by the British administrators who passed legislations from time to time banning these evil customs permanently. The most barbaric evil was the practice of Sati where a widow was expected to Immolate herself along the burning pyre of her dead husband to prove her loyalty. The custom was very popular in Rajasthan and was given the name of jouhr. The legends of the Rajputana history mention about mass immolation of queen Padmani when the army of Allauhadin Khilji breaks into the city of Chittor. To fear dishnour at the hands of the Mughals the queen and thousands of women of the city did mass immolation. The queen has been accorded status of a goddess and worshipped in the desert state of Rajasthan. English Administrator William Bentick took the initiative of banning this custom and it became a legally punishable offence from latter part of 19th century in India.

An Effigy on Hunt

Of no real meaning now
The white widowed in wail
A life of treacherous moans and pity
A long trudge through tumultuous times

The lecherous eyes, a seditious contempt
A widow in white for some redemption
Be it queen or a eighteen something they meet the same fate
The carrion of justice seekers, the social landlords
A faith of self proclaimed high ideals

Even the great books preach humanity for all
It's the writ of the landlord which comes in way
Away to a pyre she keeps her husband's head
Dressed like a goddess with a trident in hand
Not a hint of pain when she burns
The courage of her suffering made her a effigy to burn

Temples stand in her name
The goddess is revered and worshipped
Was it her choice or a force of will
A widow in white appears to disappear in sands of time

The last case of Sati burning in India was reported in 1987 of a eighteen year old Roop kanwar in Indian state of Rajasthan.

Human right activists have campaigned for equality and discrimination and have been subjected to political vendetta and various forms of torture maybe imprisonment and sometimes even assassinations. Nelson Mandela with his long walk to freedom had to encounter imprisonment for twenty years and saw many freedom fighters of South African die a painful death before him. It was white supremacy which devised and executed the evil apartheid to denounce the color people and deprive them of basic rights. Mandela's courage to stand up for what he thought was right was full of determination to change the fate of people living around him. By some stroke of luck he was lucky enough to not be targeted by some white racist organisation believing is racist ideals of all white superiority. Late Junior Martin Luther King assisted in bringing on board civil right moment for Negroes in America and it was a sad commentary on the racist ideology that he had die from the bullets fired by a white fanatic. One of the most memorable speeches to be delivered by him summed up in "I have a dream gives a vivid description of his ideals and envisions a future world without the baggage of discrimination and racist thought.

A Gauntlet of Extremes

Every man with a two fold duty
Care for family and lives of people all around him
Freedom fighters dispatched in coffins after years of torture
For ending a blot on the face of mankind called apartheid

Not with boomerang of bullets
Just with plain courage and determination to slain
Embarking on a course of curse
Throwing aside the cool comforts of cocooned shells

A tortuous ride of two decades in chambers of torture and deprive
Some to die and others to fie upon
A ray of hope kept alive by strong will and positive ends

A day in life of a nation comes
The vision of a utopian is realized
A crusade of seekers not meek
Masters of the universe meet a fate of their doing

The dream goes for miles
Taking in between many milestones
Since the time when it was born
Segregation for colour for inhumanity for bewitching poverty

Creation of the almighty spit upon
If the creation of the creator is in human
Put to trials and tribulations
Asked to beg for some decency
It's not the place for anyone to live

The racist mind and its evil hatred
Gun for the hounds asking for free living
Dragging the seekers to places of creep and creepers
Humanity is drugged and shrugged to find a place of recluse
in lonely spots.

Another stage in American way of life has been the increasing influence on white racist thought by wild west which has been subsequently fuelled by Hollywood western thrillers glorifying cowboys and putting to shame native Indians. As the ideas of making money out of land exploration gained currency it were the westernized people who wanted land for more mineral exploration of wealth on lands. The native people of these lands often referred to as the red Indians were driven out of their land and homes to make way for exploration of wealth and more wealth. These native Indians were demonized by the western press as barbaric and uncivilized. They were believed to be lacking in all thing human. The Indians were a natural tribe and existed with the help of nature at their disposal. They fought a bitter battle for survival against modern regimes who were up with the idea of bringing them mainstream. It took some time to educated the Indians about the valuable results of modern education. It's commendable the way the red Indians fought for their cultural identity and native lands.

Down with the Lot

A land owned by forefathers
White skins with whiter brains
Come for our lands, rivers forests, animals and what not
Barbaric, uncivilized, un couthed, they make of us
Some are called devil heads and some evil sun's or even black moons
Spitting upon nature's child
The westernizers force untold miseries upon the natives
Neither had we fought and nor will we fight
Now of no significance the way we lived
Forced to violence and made to behave like animals
The Indians strike hard and bad
A blood ravaged plain and savaged brains
The warring Indians and the foxy westernizers engage in blood sport
It took some time and sane belief to bring the warring factions to a halt
The Indians to look after their salt the westernizers asked to sink the differences in malt
A saga of century old duel comes to a grind
Now when on a wind its all a spell bind
A avarice on a hand and pure elements on the other.

Communism took centre stage as wealth owners tried all means possible to overrun worker interests using them to maximum benefit and multiplication of wealth. October revolution or popularly called the Russian revolution and the maoist revolution of China brought in astounding changes in the economic world. Workers began to group themselves into communes for better living wages and proper working conditions. The inhuman face of democracy was shown the true face and asking for rights became a sign of rebellious attitude deserved to be punished by courts of law trying out hardened criminals. Asking for basic human rights was construed as going against the state.

March on the Stomach

Men of hammer and sickle
Men of plough and oxen
Men of sweat and prespire
Men of hard metalled shield

Couch potatoes steal our bread
The blue gowns and velvet gloves rob our rising sun
A famine for emaciated creed
Mercy thy lord as born under moon and stars
Borne from wombs of unfortunate mothers and fathers
Sins or karma of past catch with the present
When it's all over, muscles loose the strength to break a wall
Some shillings for a coffin to hide or pounds for the grave diggers to make the unfortunate slide
March on the stomach
Long live the revolution
There happens a day when all will be swayed
A cobbler for a shoe, a Washerman for the laundry, some to tow the carcass of dead animals taking out the hides for the fashion boots
The walls of the places smeared in black soot
March on the stomach a handful of a gambol.

Men of wisdom have shown the becon light as how to improve life. The idea of non violence was given by Jain Saint Mahavir Jain. It is said that even the tiniest of the insect or a plant has life in it. The idea of non violence was used by many political leaders successfully to mobilize Public opinions in favour of independence from colonial masters. It was never assumed that non violence would act as such a powerful instrument to usher in changes which possessed the ability to change the way in which world functioned. The might of the sword was overcome by the fragrance of non violence. However non violence failed to address the issue of increased conflicts witnessed in forms of republics wanting to scede away from nations. Powerful USSR was the first one to agree to its dismemberment as under its policy of Glassnost it gave full territorial sovereign freedom to many of republics who were of different ethnic grouping. These republics took away with them many oil producing regions which depleted the resources of Russia. The present day Russian-Ukrarian conflict is all about the control of oil rich regions which belong to the erstwhile USSR but now under the control of breakaway republics. Even the gulf War of nineties and the famed operation desert storm launched to purify Kuwait from Iraqi occupation was all about control water

Seeds of Hate

The mover of economies or economics of the world
It's all about crude oil
Nations at loggerheads and world at peril
For I have the control the way in which the world moves

Without the oil nothing possible
Mobility, connectivity,
Everything revolves around me
From the aircrafts to ships to locomotives or even the rockets which go up in space
Now in trickles and perhaps over by turn of a few decades
Back to horse driven carriages and dark ages
When distances were traversed on horseback
All were advised to treat me with care
But carelessness caught everybody unawares
Fighting for it now as hard boil scramble begins
First the gulf and now somewhere else
A bag of lazy bones that's what left out of you
Crude oil as I may sound the caveman had the ambition to light a cave
But the present ones around aren't that brave.

One of the major adventure events of the last century was the conquest of Everest by mountaineers Edmund Hillary and Tenzing Norway. Many mountaineers tried their best to reach it first but were unable to do so. Many lost lives in the climb of the un vanquished everest. The spirit and strength of the human soul ultimately prevailed over physical barriers which Everest climb had to offer. The character of the human race is known by the fortitude with it faces and overcomes challenges. The race to the top of the Everest was not one for fame and name it were the wild nature's elements against the super will of the human mind.

Summit Calling

Like a child chiding with tongue protruding
Everest challenged the human might
And perhaps right as men came and disappeared some in its glacial depths
And some from its gigantic peaks
Bodies frozen in stretches of ice resembling a hot Sahara plain

Never to be deterred or to be frettered
A few men of blood and bone
Went in for the kill with an iron will
Everest will be over only then the thrill
The enthusiastic heroes began the trudge promising never to budge
As they moved up the breathe started to thump
On they moved along the winding peaks with snow on their creeks
Snow axes to dig in and crampons to hold on
One mistep and a fall into the bosom of everest
The blind of blizzards and the frozen bite of the frost
Never once did they retrace only to face the wrath
A couple of them with a snow grave to behold
The final two prowled on
Without a shrug
The last step and a winning hurrah
Who would be first to set foot on the everest
A matter of little concern as human spirit was the winner.

Sports has been a modern day invention and has succeeded in bringing together the world despite all the problems created by self doing of a few individuals who have taken it upon themselves to shape the destiny of people. Sports has been a binding and a cohesive factor in cementing the world into one beautiful place to live in. It were the Greeks who thought of the idea of sports been introduced as a binder of nations. From world conquests which and been achieved by Alexander the great exemplified by the recollection hydapses calling in this book. It was another Greek gentleman to suggest the ideal of olymoics. Perrie de Courbaton came with the notion of olympics every four years of all the countries of the world. The power and prestige of countries would be decided on the basis of their performance in the games. In ancient Greece Sports such as fencing, chariot racing, javelin, shot put, athletics, were common and it was considered a healthy way of living. It may have been the reason for so many amphitheaters found in Greece. The first Olympics were held in 1896 at Athens were the participation was low. Since then the Olympics have been made a permanent feature to be held after every four years. Olympics has become a source of power and prestige for the participating countries with every athlete trying to outdo each other for winning. Athletes with active support of their respective governments train hard for years to win a medal be it of any colour since a medal at the Olympics is the pinnacle of achievement of every sport loving individual.

Towards Paris 2024

It are the olympic times, my sweat is at stake
Training hard for long now is the time for a winning song
With hopes of millions on my shoulders there are huge boulders for the end
With a dream in my eye for setting the tracks on fire
A medal around my neck is all my crave
All the chairs have spend far to much on me
A debt I owned to my land would be repaid by a garland around my rear
The will to win move and race ahead
It's a ocean to be swum, a pointed peak to be scaled, a river in spate to be navigated
All I have is a sweet sleep of differing hues
Get up from the comforts of coziness and hit the ground
A ideal to be achieved a idea to be molded in ruins of times

Traitors have played a significant role for subjugation of the country in which they lived. Some sought to avenge long time grudge others did it for becoming kings which ultimately they did not become for it is believed that those who don't love their motherland can love no body. The unkindest cut from the past from the stab of Brutus who was known to be dear friend of Roman emperor the mighty Ceasar was to change the course of Roman history. Palaces became dens of intrigues and deceives were now practiced widely and loyalty was no where to be found. The story of conquest of India at the hand of Turks was as a result of long standing feud between warrior king Prithvitaj Chauhan and king of a principality Jai Chand. Jai Chand plotted against the warrior king only to settle scores with him as his daughter had been forcefully carried by the king. Militarily it was not Possible for Jai Chand to overcome the sword of the king so he joined hands with the Turk invader Ghori to defeat him. Had the feud not existed India would have been a country never to have been annexed by any conqueror. The fall of Bengal at the hands of Robert Clive on fields of Plassey was due to presence of Mir Jaffer a trusted General of Shiraj ud daulla a capable king resisting the spread of the British in India. Mir Jaffer was promised kingship of Bengal if he sided with the Bristish. Over come by greed he turned the faces of cannons on fort William to punch a hole for the British soldiers to set in the Union jack on the fort. The last bastion of resistance was done away by the white masters.

Moles in a Mountain Hill

Jewel of the east stood proud and strong
Land of seers, priests, and religions
Where the corn stalks greeted the flights of golden birds

And all of a sudden evil eyes of looters from the sand lands
Came in a rush to change the landscape
Golden bird was stripped of its ruby tipped fethers
Some for to resist the tide of cruel monsters

Sword of The king and a minnow
Settling pety scores the minnow bartered away his land of birth
The low one a traitor met a fate which only hate could meet
A curse from the lips of the destroyer the tale repeats in unison with the past
A trusted General of a resistor for greed of emperor
Turns the faces of the cannons towards the fort walls instead of the rampaging British
Union jack pride of the masters a fluttering insult of centuries of slavery and confine.

Two man made disasters have shaken the faith of the people all over the world. Though nuclear power is taken to be future of power generation in coming days. The giant wheel of economic progress would come to a halt if adequate power is missing to run heavy industries manufacturing consumer goods. It was seen to be coming but all chose to ignore the inevitable. India's Bhopal gas tragedy was a warning signal ignored and another one struck at Chernobyl in Russia. The limit of human greed was there to be seen as the owners of Union carbide the company manufacturing pesticides which was responsible for the leak of methyl isocynate in Indian city of Bhopal located in the state of Madhya Pardesh ignored safety manuals and went ahead for production of pesticides to make heavy profits. The resultant gas leakage left thousands dead and many more blinded as the poisonous gas diffused in air to become a killer cyclone.

A Smoky Death

The fumes spread far and wide
Air becomes a suffocate beehive
Eyes in tears and nobody aware
The killer cyclone strikes on a sleeping coffin city
Death city comes to life
Those alive scamper to be escape the clutches of pain
The death smoke from the hellish outlets
Consumes in quick succession
Eye meets the eye to line dead in sights
Run as one can for those in sleep will not ever weep
In the August houses in chambers of the monarchs
All plan to do hoodoo trick
The vroom in the skies takes away scoundrels to places of refuge
Some blinded some lamed for life
A few in crutches the remaining half in grave
All forgotten and dusted away in dunes of perished edicts
First the nuking now a smoky flavored lingering and lasting embalmed
The Greed of the creed goes on a stead
It's fast without a cast, rotten bodies with maggot infested Stink
A kink of mind to remind that pity is faraway in remains.

Little children of tomorrow would be having a world workout animals. They would all be seeing, hearing, and listening from the books written about the king of the forest, silent swim of the crocodile, oxen strength of the rhinoceros, the craw of bald headed vulture, the daring flight of the eagle, silent chirp of the sparrow, frightening bellow of the tusker, dolphins dancing on waves, giant whales motioning through the ocean's spreading far and wide. Little children would be inquisitive about the way roses, marigolds, bougainvillea, poppies, disappeared from the face of earth. The green meadows with the missing horses running with gay abandon,snow capped peaks bathed by the first crimson colored ray of the sun, the setting sun with its bright red scarlet carpet covering the green horizons with golden colored brocade. With the destruction of earth's symbols it are the tots of tomorrow who will loose in the bargain. The parched earth with deserts stretching into cities, grains for living becoming dear. The coming of computer aided technology is giving the children a virtual world where the real images like army of ants carrying a morsel of blood, honey bees working in their beehives, frightened bunch of squirrels scurrying around the house with some trees in the backyards. It's all a vision of the past with zero occurrence for the future.

Dim Witted Scrap Books

The dry depth and the faraway stranger
A rag skin hold with wild berries to satiate
No water in stretch of miles ahead
The fading vision a blurred mind
Some water for the breaths to continue

A water well, well sighted by the dimming pupils
With last steps of strength
Only to find the depths of dryness
The dark well with darker secrets
A muddle of drops in its bottom far and out
Without the will now in, the stranger with the ragskin basket fades into glory of the skies
Bald headed eagles come for their prey
Spiking the eyes first with pointed beaks
A rumpled skin in folds heckled and pecked to revel the bones
The last appetite for the carrion some crushed potions of bone bits.

When safe banks were non existent people usually used to put their money in secret dug outs. As paper money was not in vogue the range of money included golden bricks, jewelry and costly gems. As the close to the heart place was not disclosed to anyone the treasures were buried along with person who held them. This habit of previous generations was picked up by fortune tellers and crystal ball gazers of present days who put us in a spin by announcing something which is out of tune. All of us tend to rubbish these claims and perhaps rightly so as any belief in these hacks would mean having a superstitious attitude.

About a decade ago it was announced by some godman that a treasure existed in some dug out which could actually solve many of the problems of the kingdom and the first to believe these wish wash thinker were the Kings and his courtiers and the work of digging was taken up to scoop out the riches and relieve many of the problems facing the kingdom. What followed was comedy of sorts.

A Fools, Paradise

From the beggar to rich
All asked with purpose
Has it been unearthed
Wise men have been digging for days
Some sceptics were unforgiving
What are these foolish doing
Whosoever would leave a treasure for somebody
Some one from the collection on onlookers
The holy man is respected and his words true
He said go miles beneath and discover the gift
King and courtiers remarked that that would find no matter what happened
They went deep and deep
The country awaited with deep breath
All our miseries are on end
A good life awaits all of us
What that all received was huge quantities of soil each day
Then the king in fit of rage summoned the holy man
You made us dig for days to no avail
Apprise us all why you did
The holy man surprised him
If a king believes in stupidity
Then what about his subjects and people…

Life in crowded cities is proving to be a challenge, it's like having to race with time. People have accustomed themselves to living in small sized apartments with almost no associations outside their four walls of existence. Massive urbanization from rural areas is creating another alarm as this could mean a turnaround in rural economy which will impact urban lives as well.

Still we have in some places mansion style houses with orchards and vegetable gardens but to find one in vicinity is hard and now only in memories. Small children are fascinated to visit a bungalow type accommodation but now it's a dream cum true.

A House for Recall

We all lived with a luxury
Kings Mansions, Queens palaces
Huge houses with sprawling lands
Tamarind trees with nightingales still cooing in ears
Squirrels in dozens prancing around on the barks
Bunnies holed in on the higher reaches
A few yards for the plough
Some wheat baskets, a sac of corn

Vegetable section overflowed with joy
Seasonal varieties with some work
Sprouting onions, farm fresh green chillies
Ripening pumpkins, and volley of rose red tomatoes
Peas on stalks, it seemed that green world became alive
Orchards were the pick of the lot
Mango Groove in particular
It's shade in blistering summer

Small gangs welcomed the sight with open arms
They played the childhood fantasies
Bang Bang along with robbers and cops
Hide and seek where places to hide were numerous
Climbing trees to snatch ripe mangoes or hoping about to catch a glimpse of sweet oranges
It was a busy day
All play and no work

Now in small spaces
A space of fresh air comes as relief
Sky reaching bloc's piled on bloc's
Stuffed in furnace of fumes
Manicured ornaments in flower pots
Green carpets of grass
Magic Meadows melt
A robotic relegate from imminent

There are some incidents which leave an indelible impression on our minds almost compelling us to remember them. Rural India is underdeveloped and medical facilities are non existent and people pray not to fall sick. But then disease is common and many people just collapse because the means to save these helpless people are minimum.

Usually sick are carried on cots through rugged terrain to nearest dispensaries for want of semblance of medical relief. Most of them pass out on the way those lucky to survive have luck by their side.

Once I met a helpless father carrying his seven year old daughter to a hospital and the girl had barely had a few minutes to spare.

Fading Death

Father, Father, give me a gift of life
My breath goes away, My pulse fades
I want my dolls, her dresses, and hair pins
Dress me for the school

Take me to Gauri
Her sweet milk nourishes me
I want to feed it with green grass
I like the jingle of bells on her neck

My mother is away doing her chores
My helping hand now
Little brother smiling in sleep
Just a look at him

Her eyes flicker for a moment
Looking for a miracle around
Are the gods coming to the rescue
Then the final deep inhale

I take her hands in mine
Rub her little palms
Sunk in despair
The father lets out a wail…

Experience based poetry is refreshing and adds interest to the ideas sought to be put in place. In fact all poetry is written as such and any artificiality will be unwelcome and add to the woes of the reader.

Each one of us is a poet in heart and it's just a few starts we need before we start graduating into higher stages. Its more than two years since I took to social media to pen a few thoughts, a repository of experiences which I had collected in the journey of life.

To admire or not to admire is a special right of a reader and it cannot be infringed upon. We all have to improve on our past and that's true for a writer also. I wish to thank Facebook for keeping my memorabilia as it would always remind me of my quest towards ultimate perfection as I always say the search for a perfect thought, an ultimate rhyme and flawless verse goes till eternity.

Where the Heart Belongs to

My heart belongs to none of thee
In riches or glee ridden haunts
Among the very places of envy
In a teary dew filled moist eyes of a rose petal

My heart belongs to non of thee
Of a tyrant ridden ghost land
Not a soul to be seen
Only voices of despair and reckoning

My heart belongs to Non of thee
Hermit kingdom in rule of despots
Scramble for lust, a limitless endeavor
No one a winner here, its losers paradise

My heart belongs to non of thee
Where fish pulled out of water for laughter
Animal skins adorn walls for praise
Human skulls as paperweights

My heart belongs to non of thee
Of gems in kings court
Just as a jester clowning
To bring false smiles on a rued king hood…

Environmental disasters become frequent with Forests getting reduced making way for roads we may well be heading towards a green less earth with no wild life present.

Economic compulsions have made what we are in for. With no rescues in sight it's for the younger lot of today to take up fight for preserving and save what is now a minor share of what we possess.

Environmental awareness has suddenly emerged from the shadows as climate change threatens to permanently damage the set mould of climatic cycles so necessary for existence of living things.

All stake holders which includes only the humans need to put in heads that survival of blue hermit is in our hands and complacency may speed the destination to disaster

Blue Paradise

Some tiny torts with placards in hands
Slogans from some texts or googled out
Try to force a bargain
On a few stone heads

One said,save the greens
Other one, I want my blue kingdom
A more powerful spelt as
Stop bleeding the earth

They march through a busy junction
People look on
All shout in unison
Voices broken up by shrills

A green less barren desert
With thickets and spikes
Sprouting poisonous scorpions
And venom ridden adders

Living in a different world
Where water is manufactured
Food given by medicine pills
Even the air is automated

We planned it on ourselves
Experimenters warned us
Global warming, climate change, all mumbo jumbo
The chorus was loud and clear

With thickets and spikes…

An interesting incident to be shared among all, Indo Pak war of 71 was a brutal fight which resulted in Pakistan losing its East wing to advacing Indian soldiers.

There was killing and loot everywhere but some men were different from the ones indulging in plunder. They ransacked whatever came their way. Bullion, jewelery, ornaments of gold were the top choices of the plunderers.

A army man of somewhat different conscience thought differently. He set aside the temptations to make easy wealth and turned his back to what others were doing gleefully.

Advancing army fell upon the fire doused city Houses razed to ground, whatever remained lit up the bonfires They made hay while the sun shined. An interesting incident to be shared among all, Indo Pak war of 71 was a brutal fight which resulted in Pakistan losing its East wing to advancing Indian soldiers.

There was killing and loot everywhere but some men were different from the ones indulging in plunder. They ransacked whatever came their way. Bullion, jewelery, ornaments of gold were the top choices of the plunderers.

A army man of somewhat different conscience thought differently. He set aside the temptations to make easy wealth and turned his back to what others were doing gleefully.

An Innocent Robber

Advancing army fell upon the fire doused city
Houses razed to ground, whatever remained lit up the bonfires
They made hay while the sun
shined
Golden ornaments, silvery wares, never losing an opportunity

An indifferent army man watched in awe
Begotten humanity indulged in wanton search
A few lives to be saved as a gods place is up in flames
Rushing in where angels fear to tread

Pulling out a half burnt child from the burning debris
Parents already cooked in the unforgiving flames
Then he went for the holy book and a walnut frame which supported the scripture
He managed to save the previous icon

Companions jilted him, so this is your treasure
He kept quite, returned from the war and kept the relic for decades
Then one day out for a morning jaunt
He handed over his treasure to a holy man

When others made wealth, there is someone from the masses of hunger driven souls
Humanity searched for him
Long lost in folds of time
He reminds everything is not lost as yet.

Fun filled trekking is an adventure out of this world. It keeps us close to our roots or the place where we come from and finally emerge into. An uphill trek by the side of a small jutting peak, to reach the top have a view of the greens overlapping the oxen tamed fields or a catch at the fragrance of the clouds.

However the adventure is becoming limited as people queue up in gymns to pump iron to add packs. Trekking as a sport is for nature lovers, paradise hunters, and lovers of green.

I have had the jubilation of almost having trekked for two decades collecting along experiences of varying shades. All of them hold a special place in my memory.

Enchantments of a Tramp

It was a place dedicated to gods
Trident temple on a hillock
Or a revered pond where
A celestial pair tied a wedlock

Mount looked big
The climb bigger
Summers not that hot
As a swift breeze dried a perspire

In winters the walk through the
Dense undergrowth
Warmed the cold blood
Not to forget when it thundered and showers came pelting

Smiling cherry faces of hilly folks
Far from the materialistic evils
Ready to serve with smile
Hardly ask for anything in return

On a moonlit night
A local popstar with her folklore numbers
Huge metal cauldrons of boiling rice and spiced pulses
Carefree hip hop of villagers to the rapacious numbers of local maddona

Stored in memory for long
A weekend swim on a deserted pool
Surrounded by tall pines breaking with the wind

Keep the doors bolted
The grunt of a wild bear
Shriek of a robber cheetah
A slight noise in the muddy roof
Could mean a lengthy beauty...

Why does mother earth bleed from the doom Inflicted on it. Rampaging beasts of burden have virtually made it into a hell. Extinction of species is just the tip of the iceberg as more scandles come open to watch the decapitation alive. Dagota protests have caught the imagination of the environmental activists the world over. In arms against rampant commercialization of a specific oil rich basin these protests now threaten to blow out as authorities are now giving up patience and resorting to force to crub the dissent.

Cursed Wealth

Rag tag bunch in trampoline houses
Almost as a army on a battlefront
Wearing of heat, sunshine, dust
And hunger

They come in all shapes and sizes
From a three year old warrior to a sprightly eighty year
On weekends they pitch in with vigor
Harder the crack of baton the more the resolve

What for you now to drench now
Dig gold, hauled diamonds
Went deep to unfurl ocean pearls
Reached the skies to fill with smoke

It's a brute of a crackdown
Chase the busters to their dens
The inhuman pack, loboster's on a sun dried creek
They survive the assault

A few reminiscent moments
Bruised limbs, shattered noses
A limp walk but never in the spirit
Hail humanity of concern…

Grannies always hold special place in our hearts. They are heavily emotional and doting. Sometimes you may get a one with a stick in hand to punish but love always uppermost in her mind. A visit to grannies house meant that you were bound to be treated like a king or queen for some days. We always cherish the keen moments we spend with our grandparents and hope that scientists come up with a time machine to roll us back into an era where the oldies stood up for us.

A Savory in a Dream

There were some jars of those awful pickles
Giant lemons sliced in sweet and sour dessert
She was a wonder when it came to these
The taste seems to stick even after decades

On the hearth with logs burning
She spilled delicacies in dozens
Each savored to the last bit
Crunchy munch of recipes now rested in history

She was overprotective or possessive
Defending us when we were wrong
Spare a rod and spoil the child
Grannies are always like that

Silvery grey hairs and wrinkles everywhere
She aged rapidly and we grew to the realities
With each passing day she weakened
But always a smile to count the final fate

Down the decades I see a grandparent holding hand of a child
Same old warmth and a shine of care
Its humanity which wins
Grannies are special they say…

Trikuta mountains housing the world famous shrine of Vaishno Devi was indeed a beauty of a picture out of the priced nature. Unfortunately rampant earthwork of the revered mountain range has dotted the landscape of the mount with modern amenities such as battery cars operating in carefully discovered routes as huge iron monsters took over the mountain ripping the mountain into a chicken pox scarred look.

Having visited the shrine in early eighties the changes are frightening and beyond comprehension.

A Scarred Ridge

The green of revered shrine overpowering
Pines all the way and the voice of the goddess a few miles away
Air breathes fresh and clean
Simple folks in simpler attires

Down the decades
In comes an invasion of monsters
Merchants with stacks full of currency
Land of gods were aliens step in

Further trouble as huge iron gaint;ss
With claws to price open rocks
Slaughter the abound of trees
A mount looks mighty different

Look at the mount a scarred maiden
Souls in search of salvation reach
No more a small trudge
Flying mosquitoes buzz overhead

No more a green paradise
Mount of goddess overcome by greed
Now for the ultimate
A revered shrine once it was…

Lure of holy river Ganges is overpowering as it mingles the soul with the eternity. Those who have visited the holy town of Haridwar or gates of almighty know the serenity of offerings given in the evening to the river. If you haven't it's time to go there to be in ears distance with voice of soul in all its purity.

Song of the Holy Waves

Sound of waves beats against the silent pulse of heart
Ganges the holy one comes in a downpour
Washing the evil thoughts banishing the sin ridden Minds
It meanders along in icy cool stream through centuries taking along gods and ordinary

Come the evening on the banks a gathering of sorts
Humanity submerged into one whole
Rich, poor, lame and the able
Sit to watch the glorious offerings to the holy one

Huge rings of fire alight the shores
Cries of mercy drown the splash
Mercy for a doer of nine hundred sins
Ganges embraces each one as a forgiven child

Vexed souls in desperate times
Driven by desire beyond the reach
Foul the holy one
But the holy downpour comes along

Having spend twenty years hiking around the sub mountainous tracks of Himalayan foothills the sight of mountains cools of mind ravaged tensions of a commercial life given to abrupt turns in and turn on. As you move up from the moisture laden content of the plains evaporates in cool breeze wafting in from stretches of poplar trees. But there is something else in those cooled surroundings.

It's a wild guess but the snakes of the mountains can be seen everywhere.

A Maiden on the Slither

With a bag pack on the heat
Kept the fire burning
I saw one as small as a coiled spring
It was thick and hard
An adder, stopped me dead in tracks
It was basking in the winter sun
One foot on it
And the venom puch could have put me to sleep
Just in time to glimpse at the ravanishing mounts

This one seemed long and sleek
The hooded king descended in front of eyes
Retracing to a safe distance
It slipped into the undergrowth
And then the shock
It quickly emerged from the shadows
Took a hiding in back of a tree
Waiting for the unsuspecting victim

And the final one
It seemed to undefine length
It went long and the body drag was jaw opening
Good land lady came to the rescue
Hasten the step least it strikes
The leaping run saved the day
For a glimpse at the ravanishing mounts

Innocent souls have been cheated down the memory lane. However despite the trials they have been subjected to their voice of deprivation rings loud and clear in the ears of those who used their to trample them.

Pity the One

Pity the one having to bear the brunt of evils of war
Pity the one shying away from mobs crying blood, blood, blood
Pity the one asking for peace
Pity the one walking with a olive branch and a bouquet of roses
Pity the one struck by an act of providence
Pity a one of less fortune asking for dear life
Pity a one of spine and made to crawl
Pity a one made to wander for sake of humanity
Pity a one kissing gallows to awaken a sleeping ocean
Pity a one having made to sit through a night to watch his creation going to pieces
Pity a one willing to live and die with honour
Pity a one selling his soul for a few cents
Pity a one having lived with blood stained hands

A short prose on the changing faces of humanity wallowing in depths of disdain witnessed in
form of debased virtues, meaningless existence, a coward like appearence, an insect like living
just willing to be blowed away by the slightest hint of gale.

The horrific gas chambers of the universal war were devised to exterminate masses in name of racial hate. The nazi chambers of death were feared, despice, scorned,by all save the ones who met their fate in them. The nazis did away with old, infirm, diseased, non limbed infants of no bearing to their designs.

Chant of Bells

The fickel heart and it's miserable beat
When all is lost and slipping
It's the chant of bells for some sooth
It's as though the faint being comes into vein
A castaway on a lost moor
Where the sun never shines
And moon continues its shine
Chant of bells to give hope
A reason to live and none to
Defeated in purpose and lost in ideals
Whom to turn too
Of whom I knew who possessed flesh
All succumb to unknown mysteries
Chant of bells frees the lead ridden body
Takes me to joys of bliss and unknown solitude
A carefree vintage winter bird
Escaping from the summer scorch

Religious places are places of strength and soul. They imbibe the soul with all pervasive power to ward off any untoward miseries. When all is lost and gone and hope in all meets a tragic end its the chant of bells be it a temple or church which signals the coming of a
brighter days of sunshine and moonlight tommorrow.

There is nothing magical or supreme in a voice which speaks the range of emotions found in a common mind. Its not easy to find truth in a voice as there are many risks in speaking a voice of calmness .Some people have died with a true word on their lips taking care to stand up and fight for what they have said. These voices have been silenced forever and what all is heard is din without a substance in them.

With a Truth on Lips

voice of calm in wilderness
Who listens lends those patient ears
To voices of calm in wilderness
Angry collections hollowed by tiny desires
Blood soaked fields, no time for mustard stalks
Laughing heads of sunflowers in spring sunshine
Voices of calm in wilderness
Brutes from hellish paradise
Soldiers of satin sons of buried evils
Put on fires keep under a spell
Knee the last drops of a drenched lying
Barbarian's not with sabre but inventions borne out of the mind
Still, mow, the voices of calm in wilderness.

Holy men of few words of deep meaning concealing the virtues of mankind have been conveniently ignored and dusted into history without a trace. Somewhere as the odds get stacked and call for radical changes in instrumentalized thinking of a modern age the sayings of these men come to the fore binding the ordinary collectives living and leading like sheep. As sermons become headaches and wise words a chorus of tones of weeping for dead a voice of calm keeps the kindle of spirit on flames and gives meaning to a animal like existence.

Carnage of the Civilized

Skins melt on a touch
Eyes blinded as such
Two dolphin drops on islands
Isle of green crops and sugar cane drops
Become like ash not fit for wash
A wildfire bushfire on a rampage
Whirlpools of fire consuming pools drown the herds in glacial cools
Scamper to trample remains of reminiscent
A buffer called a duffer with cabbage mind
With stick in hand and magic wand
Counting the beads of rosary
Wishing for ordeal to disappear without a heed
Barren parchments scareliged instances
Defaced, decapitated, and inactivated mortals in search of morsels

Nuking of Japan during world war two may have ended the war but with a heavy cost. The atomic bombing of Hiroshma and Nagasaki bought untold miseries on the inhabitants of two cities. However it is shocking to learn that despite the harm of nuclear armaments, countries all over the world still opt for weapons of mass destruction to propagate fear and prestige.

Bricks for Souvenirs

Make hay while the wall crumbles
All convicts serving sentences break out in frenzy of fury
Brick by brick bastille falls apart
The royals making the way for a depart
Hour of reckoning for the mankind has risen from sunsets of dark
A new order makes a indelible mark
Abbatior for the iron hands and velvet gloves
Seething in seeking seculeded scions
Ordinary rag pickers and dirt kickers
Deride the ride of royals in hides
End of a dynastic saga in blood letting
Come forth horizons of different setting

French revolution changed the way the world thought. It were the french revolutionaries who paved the way for beginning of equality of human race. All the other nationalistic movements were nurtured by the ideas of french uprising. It was truly a win for the spirit of mankind willing to stand up and fight the odds with conviction.

Sword from Kalinga

Kings of kings, might of the mightiest
Sword of Kalinga slashes, trashes, human heads like pumpkin meshes
It was all over in jiffy, sword from Kalinga empowered with power
Moaning groans, hissing gasps of death, golden brocade chariots to tow away mass Mangled mortals
Voice booms from the manifolds of eternity
The termity of sword from Kalinga comes to end
Messengers of peace in every corner of the world to be send
Sword from Kalinga, a monk from a monastery

Battle of Kalinga which was the last war fought by Indian King Ashoka the great whose vast empire included almost entire Asia. King Ashok was shocked to see the scale of destruction and death in the battle and decided to renounce war and adopted Buddhism to spread peace and love throughout the world. Incidentally Buddhism was the first religion to message in peace to the world lost in senseless wars for occupation of territories and lands. The midway path which is the cornerstone of teachings of Buddhism may have all the necessary relevance as it works out a proper balance between practical aspects of living and its harmonious co existence with the self for healthy future of not only the self but of the universe.

Two man made catastrophe still hunt the minds of human race. Some Nazis were entitled as war criminals for inflicting worse kinds of criminal acts of gross cruelty towards what they called as enemy nations. The first one already mentioned in a preceding passage headed as carnage of the civilized.

My Breath is Mine

My breath is mine till the moors begin to wind up caravans
Though over the hill it's the chill of the chambers where humans are grilled
With the bit strength in mine I promise to shine
It's better to face the firing squad
Rather than be stoned in there
In those wretched hellish confines, devilish minds with darker shines
Escaping from the mesh like enclosed palms encircle some moments of grace
Head high, chest to puff, and eye to scruff
Last of the volley goes into the rumpled skin with fork like precision
A dead dragged, gagged, ravaged,
Savaged,
Castigated crucified shunned by the huns
Embraced by the guns, honour in store
To subsist in those horrific quarters or die with smile…

Water pollution has been a major factor for depletion of marine wealth. Aquatic life has been the most effected by water pollution caused by oil spills in oceans, testing of nuclear bombs in oceans, or even extraction of chemicals from remains of dead sea fish for medicinal purposes. A fisherman with all energy at his end sets out for the sea for the morning catch only to find himself to be greeted by black waves instead of the usual blue ones. fisherman lies in deep graves of the sea bed trapped in jelly like weeds which suffocate him.

A Undeserving Sleep

Black waves and my catch
A time when net was packed to brim
Fresh water crabs, trouts, crap were all in trap
Crackers in festivities
Carrols in eager by choir
Suddenly in those cyclonic whirlpools
The black waves
Catch dried by the day
Half baked in spill and out of breath
Black waves changed course
In anticipation of day
When the golden olden returns
Singing a dirge on bow
He set sail in sea of breeze
Lonely boat tossed in dragon waves
A life consumed of a net with a catch
No one ever heard of him ever again
In twilight of the moor
When the invasion of the black waves commences
A lone boat, a fisherman, and his melancholic ode

Pollution of oceans is affecting human lives save them till they suffocate us completely. Unfortunately nothing serious by way of strict international monitoring has been on the anvil of world forums which can cause a difference.

It were not only vast armies which battled on the frontiers but soldiers of vanity and treachery called the killers from the maiden army. The only swords which they had were immense natural endowments which were used on the muscled warriors drenching them of strength of the sinews. Leading many capable all time famous warriors into a well thought out honey traps which eventually out did their forces propelling them into worse kind of military disasters.

Invisible Death

Setting the mighty Thames on fire
Oasis in mid of a sweltering Sahara
A diamond stud in the eye of fire belching dragon
Black magic eyes, voluminous the honey dipped trap
Shine of thunder in fog tripped horizon's
Drinking from their artesian depths
Intoxicants of luxurious magnitudes
Of a caravan lost in whirls of Sandstorm's
Black magic eyes, confound of delight
Octane flavoured sight, they blinded the vision full
What of those who had non in store
A mistake loved to be repeated time and again, again and again
For a blurring second, when time froze on tracks of passion
Black magic eyes, unforgiving, merciless
Executing the rovers with strokes of flashes

Drop of tear from eyes of a heart
Long passed into history, in a confine of a page
When knights wrestled for a heart
Kings threw thrones to rubbish for a heart
World was forsaken for a place in heart
Love touched summits, fired ordinary mortals into legendary heroes
Time when the heart shed a tear from its eyes
Long lost in sands of time

Imprints washed by the time clock
Now a gamble, only played by the tricksters
Wonder where is the passion lost
Gone in winds, lost in madding crowds
Webbed in hate filled Minds
Love in trickles in rivers of tight fisted sprouts
Let me live in my dreams cries a depleted warrior of immense gait

Soothsayers had a immense impact on thinking of people before the coming of rationale mind into vogue. Some of them went to the extent of predicting end of the world. They may have told a truth as events of last century and the preceding which had passed were tumultuous and unpredictable.

Dream or a Nightmare

Be it nightmares
A ride on white elephant brings luck beyond compare
If it were to be seen in wee hours
The dream run would continue
Of fads and imaginations
Old grand mum's advise
Shrill whistle during night
Leading to state of penury
And bankruptcy written in gold bold
The same goes for thumping of
wooden desks
Not to be left behind the pundits join the melee
Conjuring of stars and whirlwind motion of planets
Determine the fate lines
The fault lines to be corrected
By ornamenting fingers with
Precious stones to woo the lady luck
For the will full and practical
A pack of sheer nonsense to be discarded
As the fate rolls into slumber
Efforts bring disaster
Omens, soothsayers, glib tongued, oily orators
Feed on weak, wilting, weathering,

Magical Transmissiom

The cycle of world moves in stages
First the truth only the truth prevailed
But then the change made it of no avail
As world grew beyond the oceans a new stage comes to life
Age of another epic to unfold of further miseries to fold
Time for karma to make a mould
Kingdoms of blue hermits ruled by serpent kings and mermaid princess
From beneath the layers of folds emerged horses on magic carpet
Dragons with fire wagons and mouths belching canon balls
Humans no where to be found it seemed that fairies and bottled elfs ruled the thrones
Soon arrives a dark age somewhere else
Throats slit by thousand cuts
Heights of heights the lure of the avarice so pure to be sure
All rejoice with shakes of shattering gyrations on dance death of dear without a hint of fear
An end submerged in dark waves as high as the sky would reach
The three have eclipsed into oblivion and one remains to be in pavalion
Not now but the way of the sow its speeding into fresh twilight twitched tangled strings of fortunes on crutches of the ticking all time fire

Some wayward by the way of a bumble creates a rumble only to tumble
Voices of dissent only to consent
Fake of a make of robes
In caves of bygones only a foregone
Twists of fate by a way of crates
No conclusions but just delusions
Awe inspiring only to be perspiring
Strike of truth by way of a stark lie
Prophecies not diluted by the way polluted
No way to hide but the way to die spelt in bold
In those depths only breathes of some chance lost in trance
Bitten by incisors gouged by scissors
Faint but saint, envy of hunger of deprived but in contrive
To stab, to mob away a drab of less mortal found in swishes of slahes in dashes to be found in trashes

An Epitome For A Grave

Hunger of grave by the brave
Bullets in heart in silence of sears of pain of no gain only to be slaine
Voices of loud mouth heads only foul treads
Foolish in trade more so in common of no made
Weaklings of twigs of dry wood marked in silenced hoods
A celestial voice in choice by hail to avail the whale of loads of back packs in rug sacs
Endless rims of sheets of paper in draper stiched suits fit for the murky depths in stealths of wealths
Come the aftermath reminding a bloodbath of a footpath where no ghosts of era stuck in strikes of flashes of brashes of brusied a cruise to eternity of clouds in bellows of mellows.

A epitome for a grave is for all those who have taken it upon themselves to show and prove to all that they may have up lives for the sake of land in which they lived. It was not for monetary rewards that followed their acts of extreme bravery but a longing to see their near and dear ones live without fear and trouble.

Why for a Urn to Hold Ashes

Promised deeds of humanity
Either entrance of hell or gates of heaven
A submerged soul in distress
With wearing of life and tearing of trudge over lifeless tussle
Jackals bite at rotten carcasses or hyenas into a left over
Archer of great repute but pride finds heavens in dispute
A maze in hand which amazed only pride became his bride
Handsome beyond recognition proved his premonition a sword hand to be in disband
Showers on those who search for truth put their kingdoms for sale without a wail
Picture of loyalty draped in faith makes it those sublimes beyond reach or teach

Sons and sons to hold
One by one now only a behold
War take away my bliss in a cruel hiss
Mothers wish a tearful farewell for may be a last one
Just a pray for a say from a lone heart alone without a son in hand
Snatched by blood smeared hands of fate lost in folds of hate
Wombs of mankind hail a cry without hint of dry
Lips strung together with strings of fretters
Birth giver watches sons in tons lowered into trenches deep without a weep.

In their lifetime some instances take place where it is not possible to exercise restraint and individuals indulge in acts which may go beyond their normal way. Practical thinking commands to move along the way without giving much after think to what has been done. It has been observed that boisterous attitude may lead an individual to great fall which he has not thought off.

Waxed in Humanity

Midnight oil burns lady with the lamp takes her turns
For all the friend and the enemy alike
Bandaging wounds the lady keeps on moving
Soldiers asking for drops or water for dear life
Tents rife with battered and bruised
Wounds deep and heal for keep
Saint of humans for the rescue does it without a faint
Stench of blood from the trench the holy hand mercy goddess with a midas touch
Heal as sweet as the nightingale voice
Her name goes along the bird with a choice
Not an angel stepping from heavens just hand which heals the friend and the enemy alike.

A Sail in Wilderness

Oars of boat on seashore lie in castways
Banish came and then the vanish
Loaded with books the ferry set sail without a fail
Men of letters in tatters for they never gave in to flatters
Load of books with all kinds of looks
Some with coverings of skin and others oozing with salt like smell of gin
Boat of no fortune to be tossed among the waves
Whirlpool of narrow caves which never saves
An infant brushes in fear as the element tear rips into the boat rear
Heckled to drown pecked with a frown
It moves away sway way motion

In ancient times powers of the men with varying interests were on the rise. The kings believed them and the queens feared their ill temper. All was done by the royal household to keep their lot happy and pleased. But some where jesters who came to the court of royals to mesmerize everyone with their bags of tricks.

An Age of Ages

Alone possess powers, turn blue to black grey
stream out of an empty vessel
oak tree on sands green
bird fly without wings
coins to currency chests
base metals into golden wares
worthless pebble paths ones befitting the princess necklace
make hair grow on bald shining plates
miracles for toothless to tear and chew
squeaky rats for majestic tigers
tadpoles as alligators as huge as lakes
venom of deadly hiss into honey dipped nectar
Magician pulls a rabbit out of the hat
Makes a severed head dance in hall
skeleton goes up the wall
eggs in pocket as chicks and to hens in flash of a lid
Magician in town no clown
old grey and shacking become of liking
Fairies from wonderland, elves on flying brooms
turning sky high mansions now castles of silent chambers
Magician of sorts, freezes time
dream town, no choke fumes to fume
Theatres enact the home spun classics the symphony orchestra fills the air
Magician in vanishing act, never again to enact
sour and salt the time halt
wonder man bows out.

During ancient times in India the system of schooling was based on total dedication of pupil towards the sevice of his teacher. Children had to leave their homes from an early age and stay in special schools which were away from the hustle and bustle of towns and cities. With the coming of invaders to India the system went for a total change. Education which was for a few became common and a way to succeed in life. It is the life of child which is most affected by the present system of schooling. The happy faces of children are no longer to be seen and are replaced with robots working to the commands of changes in life patterns.

A Head Full of Awe

mighty yawns on their sleepy faces
weary, tired, blown out
books seem as crushing weights placed on heads
words from the bespectacled genius put life out of the heated fuse
someone from be knighted bunch stays awake
walking encyclopedia, a luminous star in an otherwise sea of mediocrity and stone heads
dud heads throne on back benches
armed with torn paper sheets prepare for a battle royal
rockets and elastic propelled air power at disposal
as the ordeal continues, bullet for bullet comes alive
pellets fly in all directions
one catching the bespectacled on the middle of face
no fume, no fret, just a nod to walk away
in comes hammer with a cane as thick as name
swinging the staff, without mercy
spanked on backs, ones with reflexes saved from whacks
sour grapes for mercy
last bell to get out of the cell
bandaged arms, smeared red backs, firearm gangs
start day with a vigor

In Hopes of Shadow

rivers of treasures dry up like mounds of sands sunk by rushing waves
fair weather friends perish under the weight of bankruptcy
those who would swear by, now shelter behind curtains on sight
but the shadows continues to live up
a companion for all seasons
to cheer, to buck, to console
the defeated soldier, a crown lost king
struggler of decades drowned drowsy
the reflection for the caution cautious
a shadow travels alone,
seeking no crutches
as long as it erects
live a life handed over

There was a time when friends were trusted for loyalty and provided necessary moral support in times of need. All that seems to have ended and friendship looks more towards the need of the situation than anything else. What we are left with our fair weather friends who cannot be counted upon in any untoward situation.

In wee hours of morning happened to see a flock of sheep grazing on a steep mountain slope and the pen couldn't help stopping. The wonderful creation called nature has been tarnished by growing tendency of a material mind to deplete it to hearts content. Any further depletion would be the final assault of planets most brilliant part.

A Comet in Dark Lining

all of them seem to hang like clouds
crowd of sheep have their appetite
busy as bees, all of them smack at green tufts, and the mouth watering leaves
climbers on a mountain track
not to be left behind a colt follows suit
they move up the plateau almost level with mists from the clouds
shepherd with a flute on lips
blows a tune to keep them interested
notes of extreme calm to balm
not a sign of hurry, the heard goes on a merry
mountains green and open
rains lash the slopes
tiny little specks emerge in green oceans

Great roman tragedy Julius Cesar was based on assassination of king Cesar by his trusted courtiers. It was his trusted friend ,Brutus who masterminded the killing drama. Grapevine of history suggests that the killing was done at the behest of Ceasar's wife the most beautiful women of the earth ie Celopetra. Brutus plays the role of perfect paramour and his secret love puts them all to shame with her daring exploits.

Fragility Thy Name is Fair

Stooping to conquer, I got a stab near the vessel
Fragility thy name rang loud and clear
Heaving a sigh of relief she watched the last drops in fountain like motion
I give what I Have taken that too in full measure
Mercy only gods possess for the evil the blooded eye exists
in silent graves she comes in a while to wipe the green moss of the stones
there was a time when the spring sang the songs of Autumn
hand in hand she dragged the life out of me
come the winter in abundance of white sheets
a black rose greets a tombstones
a gifted black silken scarf
becomes my sole survivor
in wilderness of a period
where two hearts met to separate in a dead heat

Religious education was meant to foster brotherly bonds of peace in a isolated world. It were the wonder discoverers who with string of inventions changed the way the world would come up in future. Travel accounts now freezed in volumes of books come out with startling facts the way people lived a life pre and post inventive era.

Better or Worse

places zing hot summers, winters to freeze statues
trees stripped to last off leaves
stems scaled off to last of coverings
roots dried off salt and water
houses where justice dwells, disrobed goes through a fate line
justice as thin as air, in moisture droplets
holy flow in which choicest of sinners, wash chosen of sins
water of pristine glory, now in effluents and excreta
temples where the heaven occupants put up, stealth robber to decamp with ornaments ordained
of ordinary flesh and blood, bringing to nought wisdom of centuries
miracles worked in hypnotic spells
a stroke of fortune confused with a sermon sick living in frugal existence
seeds of ambition with watered efforts
sometimes a begging to sum spirit soul
heart of gold in iron scales
fate as good as silver lining
falls on wasted fallow
monster tree to show roots evil
contempt in weird thoughts
drop of water from the swan neck
quell deprived mind, quench tossed up ego's
daily din to rustle bustle the desire burn
inviting canopy of monster tree
where the solitude comes with a cost

There was a time when the kids loved the outdoors and played around the trees and mountain slopes with all zest and fun. A Childhood was lived to full and meant to be enjoyed that way. Suddenly this was all gone as intense competition took over and children became extension arms of parents overgrown and extensive ambitions.

Tale of Couch Potatoes

Spreading like overgrown water melon
obese kids dig themselves in
all day around with those potato fries in hands
to add aerated guzzle

outdoor games a no, run in fields a big scare
a closed compartment with the choice in hands

genius, whiz kids to confound
achievers with hard as nails ambitions
high intellect to surprise
magic with fingers a handy tool

no real back breaking load of work
a gifted memory to seal in what is read
milestones attained in short spans

tempers always on fire
need for ice cold buckets on head
work to win, perform to achieve
motto uppermost

those in slog, the dude clogs
where a super calculation could make the head spin
in generation to follow, a solution with snap of fingers

birth of civilization of wizards
but disease of spread and swell
no sweat, no toil, childhood snapped

ribbon one with the oily plaits
looks for mates to play hip hop or pebble throw
now engrossed on a screen with dots in motion
and ear splitting, screeching, sounds

Hangmen were given the dreaded task of hanging criminals as well as those who were up in arms against any kind of insanity which they thought was against their wish. These renegades later stirred the imagination of the masses inspiring them to feats of unsurpassed acts of courage and bravery.

Loop and the Knot

In sleep, hangmen ties a knot on black masked invisible
thankless accomplish in rule of will of law
I am no one to take a life

lifeless faces, waiting in steps to be hung by the loop
no remorse, no fright, the hardened ones
hit the gallows, to drive home fast and sure

Prisoners, convicts, cheats, some honour disrobes
a few tried for treason
A pray to lord, that never in wildest dream a punish for the innocent

a hangman in sleep disturbed
too young to accomplish a noble venture
singing all the way through the dreaded ritual
kiss on the fold, lever unplugged to release a life

a singing patriot, or a soldier of revolution's
in millions of years a time arrives
a hangman does a favour
Sprinkling the dying embers of a diseased struggle to a wild forest fire

From a toddler to a octogenarian
they sing in nook and corners

throwing themselves in full gear, time and again to rear
sunshine of freedom, or a yoke of bonded dishonor
Thanks my hangman
Be not disturbed in sleep
a knot tied on invisible
arouses pent up passions of a universe hindered

Pets have always evoked great deal of curious instincts in cats. It's a symbol of good luck in some sacred texts and equally held in venom by some others. In some of the revered scriptures cat is held as a sign of some bad omen which can spell a disaster. Cat's are considered as senior cousins of the majestic tiger and even related to the king of the jungle in many ways.

Feline Majestic

cat on roof, piles up hurricane of sounds
searching for pests day in and out
adventure overdone, milk in kitchen vanishes and the sleek through the slit
leaves the butter high and dry in the frost
cat on roof, dances cyclone, when chased by big, brown, baboon
moment of relax and eatables in hand disappears
when in tantrums, the cloth line all in torn rags
big brown baboon grins showing sharp claw teeth almost mugging
of all the intruders, the wall reptiles like crocs in a lake
scale the walls as high as Andes
admirable climbing skills least one falls into your lap
the roman army on the move
sex legged warriors, to scare the daylights out of the most daring
explosive packed flint guns to stop the assault
house or animal farm
they get around whatever be the defence put up
through pint sized holes
hair line fractures in walls
they uninvited guests, some as vehicles of gods
deserving place of worship up front

Child of the forbidden one is one of the worse kind of unfortunate ones as he embarks on a journey of selfless service. People around him make merry while the sun shines. He takes the brunt of punishments heaved on him. The unfortunate one moves on despite the hurdles which keep on coming at him with regular frequency. This makes him a stand out hero. His life is celebrated after his death giving the unfortunate one a cult like status.

A Deed for Indeed

do a good remembered deed
give the drowning a straw to hold
teach the child to walk by holding the fingers to watch the rocking gait
give the red cherry cheeks a smile by wiping the tearful tears
in a thirsty afternoon, as the sun pours anger
a glass of water to the unknown stranger
do a good remembered deed
the mother earth bled by thousand cuts
feeds the teeming babies
water pours forth from inner depths
to quest the throat
old stick in a forgotten corner
to be held by the bent back
old tree planted generations back
gives umbrella to the travel weary
a moral lesson to the wayward
tale from a classic, the bottom line all telling
noble minds of deeds, better off than the muck trashed, lies in buttercups, deception served in dessert's
no need of super god, or a big hearted philanthropist
just a tiny deed by the man walking down the road, a stranger in the faceless crowd
watch the unlettered write a name with a flashy grin

erect a wall brick by brick to build a skyscraper
do a deed
which remains a parting gift
worth than thousand fortunes of rust

A Expression as pure as true love is hard to come by. When all seems lost and looking for a way out of troubles its only the purity of love which will stand the test of times. The language of love signifies a world of contrasts. To a child it are the arms of the mother, to a lover a shower of happiness in darkest of the nights. As age fades away into the twilight of sunset, a train of thoughts emerges in the folds of times when love touches the strings of the heart in a jovial beat.

Strings of A Beat

waves on lonely shores touch the heart
the dying motion of the swing beauties touches
they come in violent rushes only to be crushed
lonely waves on shores hit the rock to slide in fountains
prism in brilliant reflects of the dying sunset
a thing or two about the life in glide
in youth the energetic motion of swing tide
in high leaps, the gush flow of the veins in spirits tailed up
as the wrinkles climb on the wave on the lonely shore comes
a cropper
like a dying flame rising in giant flickers
the life in times well past the prime
makes fatal bid for the unforgiving heart
wave on the lonely shore touch the heart
during high tides in neap moon nights
a time when life never hurts
will to go on in extremes
wave on lonely shore reminds of a thing

There was a time when gods messengers like Florence nightingale and Mother Teresa provided relief to thousands left to die alone in battlefields or dead in dirty streets of big cities like Calcutta. These ladies with immense responsibility carried the will of service with them. However it has passed away now as no one can repeat those acts of selfless service as greed overtaken by affinity for material possessions has now assumed universal acceptance.

Chalk and Cheese

Groping in dark, the hand that heals
leapers with hands seeping in pus
toes swelled to elephant size
shunned by houses of belong
shooed off by the ever kind humanity
in din of cities the hand of the angel heals
a mother, sister, or a nun
poverty stricken masses in doled out favours
during battles which stopped with last ray of the fading sun
soldiers half dead, bleeding corpses with festering wounds
a nurse with pounds of cotton swabs
and a lamp with a flickering flame
nurses the almost finished to life again
call them healers, messengers, or gods wonder creations
in comes the baton exchange
not any one of them around
they take in pounds of flesh for the dinar
is it that the prayers fall deaf ears
for years and years the vast unoccupied by them
it's the age of knifed angels, scalpel in monk outfits
to drench the morgues to bloodless state

It's not about love for your country, it's not about love for the humanity ,it's not love for the diseased, hunger ,poverty stricken residing in those dark shades of an igloo. It's all about a caged heart which speaks of a language of its own making. Absolutely of no rhyme or reason but somewhere the talk from the four chambered veil would reach the ears which have been bitten by cold frost or even a fungal ridden consciousness.

Olive Green With Olive Branches

Only the brave remain in minds for times to follow
little men with no big ambitions
a plain uniform, with the pet
a gun and a few bullets
no where such men of dulled senses
as the scramble for greed envelopes
in fierce storms, by the fire driven battles
courage my armour, survival the shield
a non violent soldier with hands tied
bullets in name of peace, blood spill never a craze
for a honour called motherland the will strikes the blood
eyes in tempers flayed
name of bullet, on which to bleed
passes silently through the heart which sings love songs of
tri colour
greed breed the awful creed
the enemies from within
the sea of corrupt, soil the sport
in fade hopes, a life lost to teach
culprits of the dens dark
little men of no big ambitions
master the art of savage hide
not the fortunes, for a farewell end
not a drop of tear from the one whom the shed

romped in decked elephants
the golden saddled stallions
with whips made of silk feathers
little men of no big ambitions
the love song of the tri colour on swollen, cracked, dry, lips
just a last bullet from the pet
as long they grow in nurseries
imbibing the strange lust from sources unknown
will to dangle by the fire, play by the sword, dance by the bullet

a soldier the most valued gift in planets where the angels once resided

Several have lived by a worthy illustration and the rest have just been covered by sand and gravel. It's the unbelievable mind and the kind of unseen strength it possesses that some continue to shine in minds while majority slip into oblivion.

Torch Bearers of Cradles

Minds strong, the pains unbearable
time strikes the hands which belong
my fight to live for life
no time to cave in
give in to lapses of fortunes
in my eyes the long wait
of walk by the green turfs, with flowers of springs
in a room for a view
the sinking, ship in its last throb
minds strong, times gone wrong
for the need I ask for health form the bestower
not even in wildest nightmares did the omens search
a few breaths, in between days and nights cut short by evil way
I stow the left over of a stale mind in slated fates
now only a long undisturbed sleep
awakens the salvage seeker
in the pain a sweet memoir
it's the short one with gifts
which the fortunate ones beg

A major awakening in Hindu way of invocating gods took place with the coming of Bhakti cult which changed the way of worshipping altogether. Saints like Mira Bhai showed that with extreme kind of single minded devotion it was possible to meet the almighty in pure physical shape only when the mind and spirit are cleansed with penance devotion.

Clay Devotion

on how the kings veiled in jealously suspect love for clay deities
magic palace bites the mystic wanderings
shine the lack lustre glamour
of stored treasuries fails to excite
all day around, in season or dry springs
my devotion for the god never seen or heard, scales
in minds of the practical senses
a forever mad minstrel bard and her clay idol
minds of the seated
in extreme contempt
a banish or a behead
faithful in her wishes with the wed
a silent confession to the idol carried
a burial in a wall
the ignominy of the heaped slurs
in embrace folds
temple of hearts content
ruptures in mythological powers
to take in it the most wondered, admired
of its devotee
No love for the stored treasuries, just a clay idol in hands
and a hymn on lips

Taj Mahal believed to be one of the wonders of the world stands a living testimony of unhindered love which only romatic fiction can write with aplomb. It took nearly two decades to get the love structure going on the ground with many workmen associated with the huge task of completing the love monument. The mughal emperor was obsessed with the creation and eagerly wanted that no one in near future would be able to build the one he had. He summoned all chief planners who were associated with the work and asked for their hands to be chopped least they give out the blueprint of Taj to some one else.

A Monument of Blood Drench

By the cool stream
Love image of yesteryears crops
Sandstone of fairy lands
Architect of supreme quality
Add up to the dream of a love builder
Artisans of mature beyond times
Extreme toil for decades
Love conquers time toll
Not a historic site
Neither a relic wrapped in diamond studded baton
Pure crystal love shining in reflection of moon baked shine
Love in walls stamped with craftsmanship
Neither a better tale, nor a golden feathered heart script
Blessed with eternal glow
King in a cold mow
Pair of hands that built the fable to concrete
In acts befitting the king
Live to breathe, never ever to build again

Epics of religions have mentioned the name of goddess Sita as an embodiment of perfect womanhood. Sincere and devoted and ever receptive to the good of all. She was considered as daughter of earth and could not bear any slur on her impeccable moral image. Even if an iota of doubt about her chastity arouse in the mind of her lord she thought it better to be consumed by her mother ie earth rather than live a life of pock marked reputation.

Undesired Boon

Blue heavens
Brown decay called earth
Pious men in white robes
Grey men with black
shades
Rising of the sun warm
Eclipsed by silver linings
Pure white milk jelly moon
Red in stripes, in half mast appearance
Is it a coincidence
Or a matter of chance
Birth of a new born
A gift of cradles
A wooden box
On the depart
Bloom of rose on the fine threaded
A whither on the stem
Ripe green fields of mustards spread into invisible
Tumble down of cascades of springs
Erecting barrages of concretes
To vision the surroundings
Supple limbs
Strength sublime
Tick in the beat
Rush of the pulse
Weak quacking of limbs

A slow fade pulse all well known
Is it a coincidence
Or by some conjure a truth
Morning honey in brewed silver spoons
Sprinkle of birds hush voice
By the sunset all in vain
On golden thrones
But a time
Even a rag not in sight
Fame of kings
To be blamed by a mere soul
Earths daughter
Looks for a place
To shy dishonour
In a crater
Is it a coincidence
Or a conjure

A common thing called a cur which is wished away by all has been a witness in a paradise where most of the pious human beings that ever trod on earth failed to reach. The cur had only one thing which was sadly missing in human beings. It's unflinching sincerity towards its master and unquestionable loyalty takes it to high levels of bliss and solitude.

Paradise Gate for A Cur

No one came that close to me
Even in the wildest of fantasies
A thing called a cur
Embark on the journey to heaven's
The pride of the archeror who could pick fish eye from a mere reflection
Maze might to dust armies of elephants
Most handsome of the creatures ever created by the crafter
Find the open gates of the sublime house shut
Slur on humanity called a cur
Welcomed with open embrace
And along with him a soul who loved truth
No place for the swordsman who could swish away heads with the swift strikes

Horse and chariot racing were the liked leisure time of people who lived. Horses were born, bred, to be winners in all the races they took part in. They were the ornaments of a kings kingdom. People applauded them and the king decorated them with all kinds of fascination apparels. However with cruel aging these thoroughbreds lost strength and were given a painful death by those kings who once had pride in them.

Thunder Hoofs

When the galleries applauded
Lightening hoofs overtook in clean strides
punters with bag full of coins
Wished that blue streak always flashed
A Colt of the lands
Born, bred, in laps of luxury
When it ran the mountains moved, clouds rambled
Cruel age comes with time
Sinews get weak, power goes down the drain
By the old and disheveled stable
A bunch of hay to munch
New sensation, takes over the show
Blue streak fades into the shadows of clouds
The last race, blue streak keeps up to give his best against arabian king
Claps go in waves
Blue streak with his power hoofs
The last stride, a leap to conquer
Blue streak fades into a grave
Winner of hearts, one who never gave in his last race

It's a contrast of sorts ,on one side the pristine form of earth with purity written all over it and the other shade being the polluted one which we are supposed to be frequenting.

An Opposite of Concern

When the flute shrill echoes in valleys deep and green
the breeze stills, chirp of parrots on branches hidden from the eyes stops
as if drenched in peace overture's
sweet, sweet, resonance resonates far and wide
a moment of anger escapes the beleaguered mind
hate filled head comes to a stop
the mind in upheaval looks for the notes of calmed blessings
invisible musician enchants
sweet flow of air in valley deep and green
every now and then
to still the passions of a decayed soul
peace eluded by secluded thoughts borne from devils desires
only the flute player with the magic fingers and gifted boon
brings solace in disgrace

Wood cutters hack at my bleeding stumps
Black bellowing dragons Puff mounting columns into my being
Crystal clear the oceans I bestowed
Now filled with dirt spills from demons frequenting my lands
A blood dripping moon tells a tale of rapine
A dull ash sun glow a silken sheet to make up for follies of pasts
It all began with sun, stones, deserts

Men of rustic bends and certainly no bent
Pastures overgrazed to reveal brown earth
Forests without roars, trumpets, the deadly hiss
A sky with a dripping red blood moon, sun of ashen grey
Earth a emptied vessel, gold for the diggers, silver for retinues
Metals as base as iron turned to awe inspiring pieces
Rhino horns for the honored chief, loins mane on the shoe case, gloves of alligator skin
Flog the speechless spectacle supremely
A life of a century earths robber
In thoughts of centuries to be lived
Innocent eyes, in folds to esteemed, a child not hungry or without clothes
Asks for the gift stolen away

There have been many tragic love tales all over the world only proving the sublimity of a true passion which never fades away. But all love tales are not meant to be sweet fables which end on a happy note. Most of them meet with gruesome ending only to show the pulse of resistance against love.

Classic Love

In a old library, by the old monument
Where the ancient relic's in termite eaten abounds
Walls wet with soot , perfume to nausea
Thread hanging from the once masterpieces
Love tales read over and over
Of an arabian lover, to flame passions across the salt deserts
When the tribe rule over ruled the heart
In a cool flow of a downstream
A lone pitcher floats to tell the story of desires burned by tradition's
Slave love for a throne queen
To ward off the advances royal
Sometimes the treachery of the poisoned charm
A stab in the back to tell a different story
In a dim light chamber, now forgotten tales
Now no love for the lore
Eves love a garden epic
Adams fatal a classic

What do the murmuring lips pray
language of tears in front of the placed pedestal
Scarred by black pock marks, a fair maiden for the looks which melt the passionate knights in golden armor
Weakened by curse of angels, a bent hunchback for the ramrod straight back

A penniless shivering in glacial nights, for a warm seat by the fireside
Slow cough linger in the parched throats for a glorious ride
what do the murmuring lips pray
A place in heavens among the lords
a life lived of hell and slaughter

wishes the moon as engulfs strangle
the lover of roses
for the one without a thorn
a proud soldier for the moment which takes him to eternity
aging beauty for the everlasting charm which disarms
a wretched drunkard for the nectar which takes him close to the honey pond
A blind for a rainbow in eyes

A wondering monk finds himself in the middle of a paradise where the angels are having best of their time. The monk feels out of place in a strange land and wishes that it would have been better wandering in forests of the earth than coming to a place of fiery passions all inviting to a incited one but not the monk.

Trapped Stranger

No more of the wordly sayings
They spirit to belie the hopes
In thousands of days passed by
A messiah enters the gates of heaven
Inhabitated by the ones watching the tender damsels in fiery passions
Confined to corners in blue rosy paradise
A sage, monk, a wandering rebel
Counts the times the forbidden sins committed
Lord of the land in thrones made of beaten skull and bone of those who dared the good evil
In commandment of the tongue tied nobles
Stranger in land where milk flows from the cotton pods
It rains pleasures and kisses from the skies created of choice
He the messiah belongs to inferior class
Downtrodden souls languishing in bottoms of viper infested pits
He belongs to non of us
Blue blooded, Royal heritage
On diamond specked saddles with wings of brass silver and gold

Excommunicated in exiles of the forested lands
Wondering cyclone conceives the lessons of the graved humanity
Banned from places which belonged to the lords
The wide and wild meadows with lofts of unbound snow dumps
For the lover of land a forced confine is not enough
May the godliness of creations done in opportune time set aside

Walked on a gravel path all time around
In hope of the all elusive sunshine
Never ending journey
Depth to defy the depth of gorge

Men of character overcome odds in plenty to emerge victorious. To them an obstacle means a challenge to be overcome no matter the time it takes. They are not weakened by minor distractions and are ever ready to face any situation which comes to the fore. People not born with riches make it a success only because of their will of never to give in.

Granite Humans

Insurmountable struggles asking for the test of character
Deformities of mind, weakness in physical frames
They fall by the wayside, some swept away by the heap trouble
Very very few go the long distance
A light appears in the distant mounts
Chants go up in spirits
Mind fills with courage
Riches go dry, gatherings slip in sly
A strength of regain in silence of the hymn's alien to all

Dont mistake it for the weared down heart lost in eyes deep blue
Curse of angels, the beat of humanity dies in a linger
Of vast tracts of land covered by unknown graves
People died of reasons unknown
Blue blooded or the royal heritage
And sometimes the mad whims
Faiths of centuries to bond the pearls
Is it the luck or a stroke of misfortunes
A religion of life called humanity dies in the arms of living souls
Stacked by burdens of wisdoms
Most of them all greek
Geeks follow the lore sweet in compose
Disastrous in decompose
Waiting by the side of violent shores
I hear the crash without the slightest of the tugs

Nature has love in abundance for all those who want to remain with it. It's similar to somebody lost in trances of cool times when birds of love sing together. Love has got a unique quality of tenacity associated with it which may not be seen by anybody but only those who have experienced the emotion.

Sublimity Ensconced

Open window by the sea
For all to see
Among the flow, a dear heart is lost
Bouncing down a distance
Over the mighty splash
It knows no gash
Saved it from the rough and tumble
Now lost nowhere to be found

The legend of great men who started as ordinary foot marchers for freedom found themselves galvanized into people of exemplary courage which turned the masses into foaming ores who wanted to be free at all costs.

Fitting Finale

Black scarf of doom around neck of doomed
Executioner takes another one tied in ropes and now absolute no hope
Prisoner of half burned half churned desolate of mounds
Crown of all glitters his law smitten
In stealth his wealth without a semblance of health
Ruby's sapphires of nectar drenched wines of no shine
Ordinary mortals made to be immortal
Marty's of self proclaim of no claim all slained
Dreamy end for an errand
Fall from height the neck cracks a whack heard in distant wrecks in those tiny specks

The British where responsible for elimination of a deadly tribe of robbers called as Pindaris during their stay in India. These genetic robbers had let loose a reign of terror in British India as they made travelling risky. The Pindaris killed and robbed without any remorse.

Pindaris and White Rulers

Pindaris thugs who did away with rugs
Plundered at will without a still
Carvans of royals or anthing on the coil
Merciless by the way to do anything away
Riches disappear and Pandris reappear
A decree to wash the pedigree
Law for the outlaw Pindaris a tribe out to bribe
A few survive the onslaught of the slaught
Race of past in times cast in books they rest and at best silenced

In a city stood a mirror palace with thousands of shiny mirrors for the king to catch any reflection of his beautiful wife. The king was killed in a battlefield and the queen became forlorn after her husband's demise. She could do nothing to bring herself around. All she could do was watch the mirror palace crumbling with the passing of time.

Mirror Rattle

Mirror house in vicinities
Face among the race without a trace
All in love only one for the beloved
Time flew by the wings only to sling
Hearts ruptured and it came in heaps without any beeps
King lost his crown and kingdom now in drown
Mirror palace silence in dark and murky nights
Crescent moon when in sights
Mirrors shine to bring forth a sublime
Centuries in exile of times in docile
Palace mirror a monument of precious moments stolen from
the treasures robbed from the kings measures

World's most active volcano, Catopaxi has held back its simmering lava within its mount and is giving ample time for the people to mend their ways and respect nature for what it stands for. However any more degradation will not be acceptable and the volcano will rip apart any time if it's patience is tested to the limits.

Fire Dragon

Mount catopoxi held its froth
From its eye on the sly
Witnessing horrors in showers of tremors
It helds its breath with writhed
Seething anger within its hanger
Patience all but gone and just a bygone
Burning froth like dragon waked from a sloth
Mercy for none and death for tonnes
Mount with smoke pouring fire flakes without takes
Catapoxi on avenge for some a revenge

On the banks of a river stood a love monument and a temple. People flocked to see the love monument and ignored the temple. While the monument flourished all through its time the temple rusted into a ruin in no time. Once religion was considered as opium of the masses and people took it as a refuge to seek peace and contentment.

Shine and Rust

On banks of rivers stood temple and love palace
Flocks of folks on errand to love gates leaving temple in arrays of disarray
Temple rusted in spider webs and the other sublimed in ebbs
Polished in golden tipped brush the palace revered
Temple a crumble a digest of ingest
Palace of love borne from deceive and temple yet to be perceived
One of passion other of compassion
In mounds of sand gravel and pebbles
Temple rots in trots speaking of a blot
Love trances with prances in wild dances

The power of reason has been a shining aspect of human life be it past or present. The age of scientific advancement has been the best as it led the world away from dark ages and superstition to age of scientific discoveries. The greatest scientist of all times Issac Newton made a simple observation about a apple falling from tree and came up with the concept of gravity which was the base of all future scientific models.

Wanderer Wisdom

Apple fall and world enthralls
All saw before never came to the fore
A wanderer or traveller just a merry reveler
A brain with some gain to tame the lame
Lost in old magic charm without a balm
World comes around with abound
Age of discoveries takes over, to ban the cobwebs among brush of webs
Minds awake senses to wake
New order to instill a stop to disorder.

Emperors have broken or made their kingdoms. A king is expected to come to terms when his territory is threatened and prove his worth to the people ruled by him. Kings lost in lap of luxury and merriment are a burden for their people putting them at a risk in any eventuality. Similarly a king cannot rule with a big heart. He has to show teeth when desired otherwise his piousness will be granted for weakness.

A Crown Without A Throne

A pauper with a dented saucer
Once a king of stature without any curvature
Blew away quandary of riches without any twitches
Passions in flame to be blamed
Kingdom will be doomed never ever to be groomed
Crown seized and capitol on seige
Charity heads caught in beds
Without a fight just the flight
Pauper sinned by heart and taken by dart

Little children have always envinced interest in lives. They make life worth the living bringing along with them joy, laughter ,fun and frolic. It would not have been possible to live a life without accomplishing their dreams which makes us more closer to them. Their birthdays have a special significance in our lives. They not only interest our lives but give us many big reasons to live.

A Day Remembered

Naughty gang for pranks, itch powder cramped in pockets
Plastic scorpions in shoes, chair with a broken leg to sit
quick reaction palliative with a delicious treat
needle prick for a kick
morning tantrums when in no mood
night high fever due to a nightmare
stomach cramps to escape the school hours
Drops of false innocent tears, to tear the callousness of hardened hearts
childhood full of pranks not for cranks
childhood bloom to adulthood gloom

Birthday girl proud and sweet, friends of choice and eats of heart
brown creamy forest cake to gulp, crisp cookies of mums oven lined with fluff butter to help
clown cap long and pointed and not to forget the airs around
games in store, musical chairs for mummies
pass a piece of paper for a clown act for the papas
house drowned in pulp colour
green ribbons for the curtains, blue shades for the wall hangings
big gang with molars gone, and others with pure molars on the waiting order
showpiece of the show a fancy ball for all

classmate dressed as Robinson the navigator, and the mate as red riding robin hood
little brother comes in as Santa Claus, and the birthday girl in silver coloured golden fairy
eating to hearts fill and bursting the balloon crackers
a day in birthday girls calendar ends
in a room full of gifts
wrapped in colour boxes and shine paper
dolls, dresses, for a smile
a famous one to keep forever
a candle in hand of a mother with a baby boy bathed in golden rays

The name of Helen Killer invokes the mind for tougher battles ahead which stare from every corner of the eye. Helen killer born deaf ,dumb, and blind would just not allow all the handicaps get to her. She invented a script for the blind and showed that all is not lost when you have high morale by your side.

The Sail of Spirits

What's there in the spirit
the answer for all failures
where the mind comes to a big zero
and doom thought to curb the instinct
the undefeated spirit gets you going
Soar of spirit is merciless
the unknown fate of mountaineers perishing in glacial graves
wheels dazzle to circle perfect moves
spirit kills the careless, who overestimate
ambition without spirit is dry gun powder without explosive power
disabled from senses yet the inventor gives a return
blind read from a gift of blind
but wait for those downtrodden by weights of misfortune
a little hiccup or a mess
find comfort in escape routes designed for disaster
they let spirits drown driven to early defeats
success stories carved from lives of people provoked by the flame which kept the mind up when everything seemed lost
those who live with it get to where they want
working slowly, tirelessly, without having to care the fruits yielded from slog
no matter the small gain
an inch gained
a hint of appreciation in a sea full of critics
spirit always by the side which way you want
pepper it, play with it, test it,
some day it gets you where you want

Mystic of the singing bards continue to hunt the memories of people from all walks of life. They have kept up the tradition of inspiring people to attain heights of fame and fortune. Their compositions may be lacking all the fine prints of professional music but they have managed to keep alive a rich culture, tradition, in face of rapid changes which threatens to undo heroics achieved.

Mystery Mystics

walking musicians, gipsy singers, on the land giving birth to warriors
compositions as old as sands on stretch, notes stretched well past into centuries
horseback sword fighters fought for love of honour
Bards voice rings as clear as a approaching sandstorm in freeze night air
carrying traditions in small leather pouches, travelling on humps in solid humid of the vast fold
A few alms from the patience of the ears
inspiring generation of masses, making aware the deeds done by ordinary men in armors in face of spears, and dozens waiting
Bards in extinction, to tardy to indulge in modern of the music forms
cult followers of a new fad, tales of brave dust in relics of the ancient attics
In moving caravans of motor wonders, or the long streamed ship on iron parallels
Bards live up to the tradition designed designated
A little would be uniformed warrior of future battlegrounds listens with all ears and eyes
of the deeds of predecessors now confined in rolls of times

A village was located on the windward side of a rocky slope over growing with natural vegetation .It was all fine until a fierce downpour brought the whole landslide of the rocky slope on a sleeping village. Only a few could have survived the disaster. Some survivors were extracated from the debris and thanked some bits of wind which kept them egging for survival.

A Gust to Survive

Hot balloon air swipes the wet brows
Saline thirst overwhelming, breath almost giving out
Final leap into a twilight of new horizons
I have wind by my side
Nut cracking solutions to thousand problems
A solver of many thoughts
Not a sage with a magic wand to swirl
I have wind by my side
Butted out of inns in deepest of nights
when moon fell through in mid of a cloud bursting nights
a shot of powering hoofs, on a narrow pavement
I have wind by my side
A village buried under the debris of a worshipped mountain
Night long rains moved the earth, displaced the river courses
I have wind by my side

Sunsets have always created an aura of wonder and amazement as they show poetry of the creator in swooning motions. It's more to the eyes when the beauty folds up in the serenity of a majestic vale.

A Sunset on the Ridge of A Vale

When the sun sets on the ridge in a vale
flight of birds rests in twigs accumulated
breeze settles into a soft motion
a sun set in a vale
reminds of smile once seen by chance in million dreams
of a soft voice cushioned in lullabies of romantic melodies
a running shadow in fading sunlight, like a fist filled sand emptying in a barren heart
a sunset in vale comes in between times when the vigor of pursuit of a wild goose endeavour
a shattered spliced blown to pieces fragile silvery ware
hidden from the rust eyed wonders which beguile, betray, be Knight
A sunset in vale, bright of colors in brilliance of shades
Stab my heart, a sin to play with the fragile silvery ware
bare the sinister of the intentions, in the mudsling a embittered soul cries foul
no one ever died for a heart in cries
lovers of centuries born since times
a sunset in a vale drifts into a soulless passion driven instincts
Just betray a heart, don't ever play with the soul
a fade of a vale drifts to stem the swell of a wild fire surge

Greatest of the empires have faded away with times leaving no traces of their greatness and emperors who thought that their names would be itched in memories have been forgotten. Greatness is not about those who sat on biggest of the thrones or brought the whole world to its knees, its all about the way an effort was made to provide some thing by way of acts which were looked forward by eager eyes by all those who thought that from somewhere the hand of the creator would find its way into their lives making them free from all ills and sufferings.

A Time, A Moment, an Hour

No matter the time, moment, hour,
a time comes when the eclipse comes
the might of romans, the grandeur of mughals, the lustre of the British
Time a killing act, a young man thinks he can dodge the inevitable
In a second the lives lived, in a minute the joys overhauled, in hours a centuries of long tiring wait overcome, in days a time arrives to revisit the sanctuaries of sacred lost love lasting, in years the wait belongs to the one who sheds the sorrows of partition to the winds, in decades a forlorn of a eyes open sleep see the prince charming on a mount borrowed from the historic, in centuries a lover of mirages in deserts of serpents and scorpions comes alive to wish see a maiden draped in Clifton's of a fairy unseen in lands of caravans and string camels
a time, a moment, a hour
a spirit goes through a mountain top
setting the summits of passion on fire
a fire in hell with no body to help
masked in ugliness never seen or reflected in mirror
a fear envelope to rope the delicate of the hearts
count the deeds, the viscount in life lived on misdeeds
a river of fire to cross, the mouths of hungry crocodiles in eager await

birds of prey wait for the fleshy piece to be hung on the alter
a time, a moment, a hour
to think of humanities washed down the shores
cradles put to graveyard sleep, giggles piped in deep never to come again sweeps
No one for care, but everybody slams in for share, only a few for a bare
a story of civilizations drifted in time ablaze
no one remained to tell a foregone tale
Romans beg on streets, Mughals hang in wayside corners, the British ask for impoverished favors
a time, a moment, a hour

We often don't want to see the giving of gifts which come naturally to us. It's of absolute sense that these gifts have been able to give lives a sense of purpose, and making the truth of human life cycle a truth possibility.

Invisible Hands

Invisible hands give in a plenty
water for the plants
fruits to nourish
a boon called a life
Invisible hands give plentiful
Partners of life to walk hand in hand
sweet little buds to cheer the dull moments
Friends through thick and thin
Parents to run errands from pillar to post
Invisible hands give a plentiful
Heat of sun to warm in still freeze winters
cool breeze ventilates in summers of tortures
tip toe gambol of a rain come peacock
a coloured wonder to bright the spread of horizons
Invisible hands give in a plenty
a ticking brain to think
eyes to fill in with pleasures
hands for the making of idols to store in worship homes
Sensations for breathing in the wise sermons
invisible hands give a plenty
angels hands for cure, men of flesh and blood who were blooded for humanity on altar
invisible hands give in a plenty
iron willed mind to stem the unfortunate tides
Blind with patience to live in dark
lamed to walk on crutches for a period
cursed the luck, who feign
hands that give in a plent

Its fascinating to hear the voices of free birds hanging about in the skies and singing away to glory. Birds have a unique way of communicating to everyone about the way they lead their lives which is free from all kinds of stress and strain which have almost become inseparable part of all of us.

A Voice in the Woods

Voice in woods
Just too good
Shrill the melody
It's all novelty
Whose the Nightingale
Or a magpie
Sun brightens
To a radiant hue
In the vastness of blue
In rest or extremes
The hunting echoes
Heart sings, mind lingers to a cling
Voice in woods
Its too good
Is it a nightingale or a magpie

Humans have always lived with pride, boisterousness, and sometimes a tiring brag. Little is known about the end of mad rat race but the momentum of the race is ever speeding. The race brings to end the purpose of life which is deep in essence and thought. In a cut throat living it are the ends which matter leaving means aside.

Who Am I

Who am I
a limp of a walking shadow
a speck of lumina in a star filled moon umbrella
a fish with gills scratched when out of its abode
who am I
a unsuspecting victim
a lump bag of a disease about to happen
a crumpling rust laid pillar
who am I
a child once
who smiled with natures wonder
laughed with shine
played with no whine
a romantic youth
certainly given to temptations
who am I
a wondering sage
a sauntering monk
a hand of a healing wizard
who am I
a prisoner of dreams
a mammon reveler
a fate puppet in a fateful fait
who am I
a rouge of colored images
a bent of a rainbow in the sky

a lurk of a ghost footstep in a wood
a lost footprint in sands of time
a giant who once lived
who am I
no one knows not even the self
who am I
a perspire on the brow
a rocking stone in a gust filled tempest
a rock with rubies in its depths
a simmering vent with a pour in
a shadow, a luminary, in the star filled moon overhead

On a holy piligrimage to a snow bound peak some piligrims were caught in a snow blizzrard. A old and wasted wooden log came to the rescue of the worshipers. As long as the wooden log burnt and kept the heat going the trekkers on way to a religious journey knew that they would live for another day.

Log Life

Mesmerizing red flame heat from the burning logs
warms the blister frozen numb fingers
The wind from the passes carries along with it
droplets of frozen dew
Heat from the red flames comes to the rescue
Circulation thumps down, pulse beat fades
Whole frame trembles like a branch in a storm
who else but the burning log to the rescue
The flame heat settles the racing stream
puts in a deep snuggle
a poor little thing as a log
with no resemblance
a waste in a store corner
when the dip starts
From a top the rugged peaks
full of white cream smearing the peaks
gusts not exactly lusts
a burning log as a companion
to keep the night going

PART 2

The book has been written in two parts the first one contains some meaningful paragraphs which are meant to explain what the poems are all about. All these short paragraphs take out important events which have happened in past or near past. Broken fist is by no means a chronological summary of events taking place in world history .All the poetic contents have been derived from events which happened and impacted all those who read them. Not only the past but instances happening not so far away have also been taken up as poetic material and written about the way it was thought best.

The second part of the book is in one whole continuity with no paragraphs sought to explain the meaning of lines which follow. The stream of free flowing poetic verses with deep meaning to the words is the essence of part 2 of the book. The language of the book is sharp and to precision keeping the elements of detail well away which would give the book a look of pure fiction.

Many of the short poems contained in the book are of common people and little incidents which keep on happening with them to give their life some meaning .A poem about children playing in a park and trooping off like a train by making engine noises invokes memories of childhood days in the minds of readers. One of the poems titled as Smokey Joe is about a gentleman overtaken by nicotine addiction due to lengthy bouts of separation he faces in life. He is respected and holds a lofty position in life but is unable to come to terms with his addiction which proves fatal for him.

Poems such as wind stealer about a stallion who won hearts with his speedy hoofs is given a painful death when it gets sick. Similarly Milk robbers is about ill treatment of the holy cow throughout the world as their owners drive them out of their homes and bring them back only when the cow is ready for milking. Dry honeycomb relates to the stealing of honey from wild beehives by thieves. All these short stretches of compositions reflect the bane of animal cruelty now so common and found everywhere. Dreams on wheelchair is about the agony of a small girl suffering from disease and confined to wheelchair for rest of her life. Hills brown skies red introduce degradation of earth and its environment. Hills are supposed to be green and sky blue but the rampaging burst of economic speeding have turned the crop rich fields into dustbowls so similar to the ones written by TS Eliot in his epic. In hunting love doves shows the hate of humanity towards love in general and drives home that still the minds are filled with poison and venom. The way of living shown in solitary vagabond where all he has to care for are is possession of free wandering without the chains of attachments which all us are all living with.

Jingle of the Oyster Shells

it warms, passions the sleeping beauties Who else but the oyster shells knew
of a heart desire hidden from the world
who else but the oyster shells washed down the beach
knew of a dream buried deep in the being
who else but the oyster shells washed down the beach
listened to a whistle out of the soft lips
who else but the oyster shells washed ashore
come to peep deep into a sleep
who else but the oyster shells washed ashore
sing a song close to the ears where the din shuts
who else but the oysters washed ashore
come close in coming times
who else but the oysters washed ashore
ring out the bells far and wide
who else but the oysters washed ashore
knew a companion lost in the madding crowds
who else but the oysters washed ashore
ring to ding a sing in a fling

Walk In

Someone just walked in
In soft toned voices
Set a heart on a passionate drive
Blew a wind into a life
Someone just walked in
Days gone light, nights don't bite
Lonely walks now no longer
In a song the voice gone merrier
Jarring noted replaced by sweet nightingales melody
Somebody just walked in
Peace returned in moments of solace
Weary mind comes to a rest in cool blue shades of showers
from peacock unfurl
Somebody just walked in

Infants Curse

In a crowd, the eyes look for a face
Teary eyed, a wonder child
Crying for papas hand, mummy's bosom
Unwanted child, a birth in trash cans
Eyes in a crowd look for someone
Heartless people, in heartless ways
Go on endlessly
Never the thought of a shiver
Eyes look out for someone in the crowd
To atone, a Abulation, in a stream
Cries of a teary eyed, cry out in the silence of the on rush
Pure in prayer, the slayers of innocents
Faces reaped in sins, harvested in cruel seasons
Those put to sleep by the false worshippers
Lives snuffed, in trash cans
Eyes look out for someone in the crowds

A Pilgrim Wish

When the temple bells ring in ears
A picture emerges from the fronts of mountain ridden scape
ways through the hillocks, with a river by the side
when the temple bells invite
Curbed by the fate cruel blows
In the mid of frightful nightmare
which hints at the undesirable
A unseen calamity, a un doused fire in a non calmed prod
a sense of belong, a barge of forceful push
a dip in the snow filled stream
which sinks the flow into a still stature
pure in body, and the wavering mind jitter
The echoes of the bells
Thrills the everlasting serenity as the senses sublime
into a lifelong trance
When the temple bells ring
Humanity in chorus, in a show of peace harbingers
flocking in heard or a flight of birds
rush in to climbs of distances
eyes vision a journey
in snow capped igloo shaped domes
a pilgrim prays endlessly
when the temple bells ring

An Endless Search

No savior, no messiah, no saints
just images of floats
constructed in minds of rickety frameworks
scattered souls search in vain
treasures not to be delved
ages gone by of those
saviors, saints, messiahs
No need for a wreck burnout
Through a rocky loose pebbled gravel
a troll through a pine yard
search limitless continues in the way
of those saviors, saints, messiahs
Time when in vices a content found
Living a den of secrets for the young brittle
saviors dressed as healers
dart shoot poison of no heal
wondering in a mind not awakened
immaculate in dress and Savior in speed
messiahs pour nectar of web traps
spiders of mere exist
with passivity as a form of persist
life of honey, in a sweet cauldron
now in a ladled potion
a long tasteless brew forced into a gulp
where are the saviors
messiahs in long bush hides
saints in sonorous sleep

Rideback to Belong

Humanity goes in vain
Color of blood in white frozen milk
Darling of hearts the jewels I adore
Color of humanity goes in vain
Blood spills blood
Brother as sworn enemies
Ego the killer of mankind's
Civilized blunder a mosaic of colors
No shades, a motif invisible
Color of humanity in vain
Trumpeters of destiny
Who cried with elate
As they fisted the skies in a clasp
Color of humanity in vain
Errored to perfection
A song of peace for the chanting
Drops of rain look like diamonds from the skies for the belly filled mortals
For the land of invaluable values
A history rewritten, a religion foregone, a repository of cultures forgotten.

Curse of Age

A king gives up his treasures
For the fading strength, sagging vitality
Golden locks in braided hooks
Wretched silvery hairs so dull
A king gives up his treasures
Bring a wise from the fertile land
A crystal ball grazer to roll back time
If not them a magician to give a few moments of relief
A king gives up his treasures
Verve in voice, a sword which never knew fear
For whom the kings bowed on the alters
Maidens from heavens waited with open arms
A king gives up his treasures
Magic potions to cheer up
A witchdoctors spell to do the trick
Some herbal condiments jelled for the elusive dream
A king gives up his treasures

Words of Mindless Wonder

A hand without a fate
A eye without a lusture
A heart without a tear
A mind without a feel
what are these
symptoms of a death climax
or the signposts of success
a pocket without the shillings
fingers without the rubies
smooth crane necks without the studded diamonds
a voice in anguish without the mad cry
a sob without the silent suffocate
are these a hand without a fate
cruel masters in stallion driven coaches
hunger filled bellies without the need to savour
chest filled fortunes without the locks
the hands without the fate
Whose life, a mirror scattered in directions
what's the fate of a hand without a fate

Wind Wisper

Only the winds knew my desires
couched from disaster eyes
buried in chests of backyards
Almost snuffed in a dumb heart
only the winds that blew knew my desires
of fortunes decked on a kings crown
or is it a merry song of hidden lust
or with wings in courts of cupids company
only the wind that blew
It rained love, rivers drained passions
Silver linings meant a glance through a veil
only the wind that blew
let the sweet sultry sleep seep
Opium of existence, a thread of existence
only the wind that blew

Blood and Flesh

A few good men stood on the way
Weak of strength, strong of will
In summer heat or biting winter chill
A few good men stood on the way
No heroes from rich mythological legends
Nor the golden throned religious figure heads
Men of blood and flesh
A few good men stood on the way

Omen of A Rumble

Does the rumble mean something
A foretell, A soothsayers saying coming true
Elements long forgotten
Signs no longer shine
Superstitions don't impose the burdens
Does the rumble mean something
A time when the forecasts were predicted true and lasted
A floating long lost in sea of waves
Meant a thing or two
Does a rumble mean something
It thunders big and strong
Not a drop for the brown basins
Lively heads droop in a ever calm
Gold harvests in dust granaries
Does a rumble say something

Heart for A Guild

Only the cruel heart knew
A hand which slid when needed
A smile ensconced in depths which drowned
A long last sentiment which flattered to deceive
Only the cruel heart knew
A sweetened brew, coaxed by the hiss
A tear in form of a cloaked fork
To knife the evergreen wish
only the cruel heart knew
For a few guilds
or the winsome coins stacked in gunny rugs
only the cruel heart knew
Mind devoid of the wishful think
Stashed away in cool slumbers
No heart aches, no fretful heaps
Live to kings desire
Die in arms of a gold rimmed decorated
only the cruel heart knew

Dusted Saplings

A great old beard did a wonderful thing
Dug holes in earth to plant a few mango saplings
First my grandfather. Then my father now the little rascal
For a swipe at the ripened juice bulbs
Bless the soul of the great beard
A orchard for a inheritance
King of fruits mangoes as bounties
Of all varieties and shapes
From the county delicious
To the sugar rich Alphonso
Then a sad thing happened
Real estate shot up
Orchard yielded a sum beyond dreams
The great beard became more greater
Mangoes forgotten as currency fodder gladdened
Now in a basket a dozen carried to remind of the old days
When a orchard shined bright and sunny

Two Brats in A Fair

A little girl and a brat out for a stroll into a country fair
No big giant wheel rides
A ride on a camel back
Some fun with the sloth bear dance
The fun continued as a chimp danced to the tunes of a flute player
And for a final touch of class the bout of a big fat mongoose and a slither beauty
The girl and the brat got excited and soon the hunger ache overtook
No burgers, not the stale hot dogs and never the sticking noodles
Fresh maize roasted and garnished with lime juice
Green apples and not so ripe pears
With a pinch of salt and red chilly
As the sun sets the fair closes
The brat wants more
Little girl goes for a sleep

Stroll Dream

Jumping jack found himself on a mercury surface
Heat dried his skin
off he escaped to moors of mars
The air suffocated him
Then to a land of rings
The vastness blinded him
Finally he found himself on Pluto
He virtually froze to a statue there
Opening his eyes from a dream
He found his ears coaxed
off to school
Cried a usual voice

Wondder Head

A little head to hold those awful oddities
Addition proves a stumble
On a subtract a bumble
Multipliers fox me
Division a Everest to scale
Common multipliers a nut to crack
Fractions split the brains like a fraction
Data handling to hot too handle
Logs do a logjam in the mind
Shapes of all sizes fly over the top storey
Never got a theorem as clean as a whistle
Progressions a wonder of world
A box of instruments as mines on a battlefield
Give a break, let me do what I can
A field to play, with a bat and a ball
To run in open winds, with fresh ideas
The hard press, not so handy
Ambitions stretched beyond repairs
A victim or a dulled reflection

Contrasting Ages

Walking down a path often travelled
A stream to follow me
Few of those floating sketches chase me
Caught in a shower in a violent downpour
Drenched to the pockets
or a slow ice rain
Freeze gusts on a frozen landscape
Tall rangy pines, the fragrance of popular leaves
Paddy fields overgrowing the pastures
Wheat baskets under the blazing sun
Yellow mustard buds singing in the wind
Of the blurring contrasts
Smoke filled infernos
Armies of mechanised four wheelers
Souls lost in an alien world
Where even water for pennies
Pure breath a precious gift

Canine Bark

I had a terror in house
An Indian Shepherd from a nomad
His name spelt an earthquake in neighbourhood
Caesar was a name destined to live in glory
Friends disappeared, enemies nowhere in view
Robbers kept at bay, thieves some distance away
His jaws opened with aggression, from the heights it leapt to surprise strangers
It hated one place the kennel
It broke open chains
Freedom was his rain
Caesar kept us busy
It sunk canines in legs
People came charging at our gates
We promised them free injection dips
A total of seven in number
When in anger
it frowned on the masters
Even they moved in suspicion
Tale of Caesar ended
When it ate up a slither
A rogue in neighborhood came to an end

Soldiers Dairy

He cried like a scarecrow for a toy gun
Dragged his feet and at times stomped them
Finally all of them gave in
All time around he now takes pride to fire bullets with his mouth
Digs tortoise like defence to ward off enemy attacks
little hero takes his ambition to a battle
Amid the whistling pellets and raining bombs
Warrior charges through the smoke screen
A handy toy gun by his side
Soldiers gun the grain of his existence
Sweetheart to his dear life
With it by side
No challenge is big enough to overcome
Some thought of a Pen in hand
Few had books to boost
What a soldier had was a toy gun
and a life to give

Coming Together

Times gone by when houses where homes
Grand parents, uncles and Aunts lived in co existence
Cousins played pranks and time flew by the winds

infants bred on the lap of Granny's
Learned to walk by holding finger of the great beard
Life moved in tempests with a smooth sail
Elders pitched in with advise
Experience of the wise council was all the advice
Oldies banished into Cheshire houses
left to fend for themselves
In a rocket age the nuclear takes over
Lap of granny missing
Index of the beard long time forgotten
In crutches Infants fed on as artificial human hood
Padlocks put on the doors
off they zoom into market worlds
Green fodder rules the roost
Sea of rats lost in a rat race
Chasing a dream which slips from the shaking fingers
Thatched hutments where the times passed by
Summers so cool, winters passed in Wool
Now in square yards a life to be lived
In hush tones, age of practicalities
Down and Drown in a period of nuclear age

Republic Lost

Chatter of gunfire
Hopeless humanity in severed limbs
Voices of hope, sanity, freedom, lost in the chatter of gunfire
All collapse in a pathetic heap
Men, women, children, of a ordinary stock
No royals from palaces
Nor kings in flowing robes
Masters of the world, kings of universe
Inflict miseries now lost in memory lanes
In somewhat different complexions
a kind of a different kind
Zealots of fatigued minds
Take charge of the purged remains
Is it a kind of a giant war
Peace of mind far stretched
To insecure and fright daylights out of the harmless
Wretched chatter of gunfire once again rules
From the ages of Socrates
Who drank a cup of poison to fight the wishers of darkness
Unknown seas of less known who
suffered fate of not their doing
Time to recollect the destiny of a jewel of east
Ruled, ravaged, and savaged
Plundered of riches
Surrendered to the gleam of the metal
Freedom a thing like a Kimberly stolen from a crown

Toy Train

Fatty one pulls the bogies in a haul
Hundreds of them behind the streaming engine
Each one trying to keep up pace
Express train whistles off in a park
Each coach holds on to tracks to avoid a derail
Front one misses the line to go down in a trickle
Rest of them come down like a ripple
Fatty the engine last to turn turtle
Never undone the high spirits spring
The train throbs to life
Mimicking voices in whirlpools of
laughter
Innocence written in depths of minds
Train whistles to refresh

Splash Without A Dash

Masterpiece without a splash
They have turned forests into fire lands
hunters with guns aimed
black soot blinds eyes
invading houses invites ire
a place for a nest
twigs are scarce
hay so rare
full plum green fields turned to sand plains
mirage of trees appears to eye of a desert weary caravan sit
on
just for a shelter
vastness of space limited
rise of morning sun without the usual tweet of a sparrow
cuckoo in woods missing
hunting melody if the Nightingale a miss
cool, clear, skies
without the ornaments dear
a masterpiece painted without the color splash

Wetland of Dreams

An eye for an inspiration
Some to die with prespiration
Tall and erect it stands like a oak among the pines
When time wines away in depths of faded shine
Dust of feet dropping from the carrion seats
Rest on stone Boulder sent to shoulder
Oak to soak of withering now a weathering
Wears and tears of time machine
No more an awe of wonder just a sultry ponder
Place of rest for birds of paradise from long reaches of solitude

Ships of Doom

Tossed among the blue whale waves coming in hails
Thunderstorm on the lash with a bash
Navigator or predator for the coming times
Search for some pleasure unknown, new lands in horizon of the eye
Some for plunder others for surrender
Pirates from the thug kingdoms in holy domes of popes
Embedded on the skins of slaves shins written on parchments of dried animal prints
Some mad angel in a fair of fairies in merry of mermaids
Toils worked out without the coils
A wind up to veil the sins of sons of devils promises

Forbidden Pleasure

Drowned in spirits of devils make a rusted relic of remake
A kings life a beggars liking
Once a console now a soul without a fowl concomitant
Legacy of brag with swag and now a drag
Sipping away to bed of thorny sleep for no body to weep
Flow of the spirits to keep in spirits
A day without the holy nectar in nerves to unnerve
Possiblity of extremes so near the end for amends now a forbidden commends.

Home Coming

Eagles sit on cloud bellows
Green growths put to the gallows
Avian cry for shelter in swelter
Soft twigs for aching palate made a far reaching waking
Summits of everest my wings take to swings
Wetlands in sights for spots of tranquility
Antiquity in vicintiy sharp eye seeing from miles ahead
Bands armed with choppers for droppers
Wetland a dustbowl of fallow mud with only sludge
Tenants of short stretches on alien lands with people of paper weight debased virtues

A Sunrise

Head on a boom tread
To be shred
Aching heart with shallow eyes
Felonies come in minds of feeble ever so faint
Thrown away in debris like motions
A punish for the banish for no one to tarnish
From the bits in slits comes the fleets of adams eves
Flowering in garden hustles in sweet bustles
Sea of humans raised to be praised out of the razed.

Unsung Heroes

Rearing a fawn by holding him close
As a gardener waters a sapling to a plant
A small thing who never new how to walk
now in a wreath Garland
Pictures of a unsung hero hangs on a wall
Cut off in his prime
When call of romance stills the mystified air
Walk away to lands not of his own possession
Battle to the last, fight to the last man
Riches not his religion
Arms of the beloved lost a distance away
A few drops of blood lost
in the mindless saga of sacrifices
Possessions so dear gone
Seas of humanity squabbles
Noises of humdrum
Baton of the royals
Specter of the nobles
A unsung warrior rests peacefully
In the arms of a mother

Mind Follies

Will and always
a poet in heart
rotten carcasses in fibre torn caskets
a no care in eyes
some wise rolling in rolls of wealth
scoff at the words
bluff the omens unseen
from four walls
a room without a view
pass the gestures
onwards to a stream of shadows
a fickle headed demon
chases the dreaded monster
to the last limits of hell
wise men in wiser council
conceive to deceive
think of a banish never known
perhaps a cup of sorrows
or a blooded framework
creatures of alien stock
always shock
always in sight
times in float

Last Breath

Let the secrets lie where they are
in deep hearts where the winds pass by
living by the flame a life
torments come as toss ecstatic echoes
In safe couches
From the fires of brandished
Or the wiles of guiles
Secrets not of a broken fist
Or a spring which never fountained
like a mount extinct
in deep crates the simmer
A small twirl in an ocean
Bonds of eternity
Kept the passion going
Without a hidden intent
Secrets of love lost
In din of times
As madding crowds engulf
A pure one of belong
Holds true to the last breath

Wretched Fate

Voices of insanity fall on deaf ears
Cries of punished sins undone submerge in four walls of a cell
Born under the sun
In arms of the earth
From the wombs of poverty
In cradles of hunger
where the sun rises to remind not to blaze
torn apart by fate omissions
Strewn aside by holy a misses
A time for the flightless kiwis
Stranded on beaches of a washed shores
Squalls split spitfire
fortune revelers dance in wild weird wonders
In high tides a pirate from the doyens of heaven laden feathers
Gathers to father a unseen adventure
Knights of no real being
a bow of only a row
An executioner of tow
Scarlet scarfs suffice
Nothing succeeds the proceeds
a tale of broken rose
With leaves apart

Life in Text

No religion to follow
When life itself becomes a religion to follow
in a course more dearer than a collection of thoughts
every hour a lesson
for every day a different sermon to comprehend
eternal peace some refuge in four walls of sacred houses
putting to desecration a temple called life
crowd gatherers on a collection hunt
a true reveler, life a faith
chapter of experiences the holy books
yearnings for will to live
a skill of being alive
rainbow of colors, without the shades of dark and grey

Kite Fliers

Kite flyers assemble as winds sing softly
Rolls of string polished with smashed glass fibre
Party gets going from the scattered roof tops of skyline
Looks like pearl harbour carpeted
Birds of various sizes and shapes, soar into gaps where ever found
Fliers tug and pull
In a match of wits
One kisses dust in mortal combat
Goes floating freely like submarine submerged
Last one standing in lone skies
Till the dawn strikes
Spirits in soar of a kite
Winds the opportunities

Saint of Love

A saint called valentine
Did a sin
Saved lovers from bows and arrows
Or the piercing fences
The love struck birds
Fled to him
Religious thrones got the wind of it
Popes of fate
Seal the fates of star crossed lovers
A love shield
Burned on a edifice
In full view of the ones whom he protected
Legend lives on
A day to remind
Heart knows no language
Utterances or follies
Only the one
Put to the sword
Guesses the sweetness of a poison inhaled

Damsel of Grace

Finally had a glimpse of many hues bunched in majesticity unseen
Maiden of beauty
Queen of grace
Like a worshipped deity
It emerged like a boon in front of eyes
Fumbling for the lens gun
To capture the moments in golden frames
The shy beauty melts into undergrowth
Perhaps some other day when the Lady luck smiles
I watch with awestruck admiration
Creators creation in times of fortune moments
A brush of paint to picture a portrait
Embedded deep in a forever vision
Perhaps some other day when the Lady luck smiles

A Different Mosque

In the heat blaze of mid June
Or the chill of December still
The hike through the lone furrow
A sound of a gurgling brook
Is all what the heart cheers for
Pure flow from the sources invisible
Eyes give away the hand held patience
As the nectar from natures arms
Reaches the throat dried
A place often to be visited and seen
The brook I passed on way
Saved me a thousand times
Gave rest to a ached frame
A place of breath to wandering mind
Never again a sight so soothing
Or a place so religious
Lone brook with a hush as it meanders along pebbles
Steps died down from the jaunt
A few to leap to save the spirits

Traffic Square

A shadow hidden in eyes
Like a tear drop holding its path
Forever in heart
Never faraway till depart
Remember the day when you held the walls to walk
Trotted to school with a tiny school bag
When you said the word which continues to drench sooth ness
Had enough in kind
But the inborn bind
In millions comes a hero
Living for others
Faceless masses called countrymen
I don't wish to inspire
Neither I want to aspire
I chose the journey destined for a few
Even if one among the countless
Goes the way I went
The ailing whom I left behind
A pardon from the unsung hero
Don't quail never wail
Those who bred me
The steel hearts
I will continue to live in dreams
For in birth I saw gods in forbearance

Of strained patience, pangs of cruel separation
I am who I am
A soldier of destiny
Live with a soul mate
Called sacrifice
For a breed called countrymen
FOR A BREED CALLED COUNTRYMEN

Written in memory of Captain Tushar Mahajan. An inspiration for generations of
Indians to follow. Let's keep the spirit of the departed hero alive.

Living Stench

Smoke, smog, or clouds
Black belching dragons
emit fumes into vast expanses
they conquer without oppose
unruly men go on and on
Fields into fallows
grasslands into desert lands
peaks into lava pouring fountains
lush green meadows or dry patches of thorns and thickets
arid, humid, and consuming
the air stifles
wafts of breeze almost rifled out
a pair of thirst driven oxen
stumble on wide open cracked craters
with hands folded and head bowed a prayer falls on deaf ears
A forlorn patch arises in the acid pouring skies
are the prayers starting to ring
for days they hang about aimlessly
smoke, smog, or clouds
the minds imagine

Cruel Eruptions

I knew about a yard of pines
where the murmer through the leaves seemed a drift of feathers
the spread of green acres all sprawled
They almost seemed never ending
A few years back that happened
Now with stems tranquilized
From the roots up to the shoots
the wonder boys of nature wind up
In the pine yards the dance of the hues
the flutter of flocks
mellowing of the rainbow on the snow capped hillock
the majestic bow of pines as the wind whistles
Rapine of the green pastures
modernity erupts on face
greens go for a walk
capital kings design the curtain fall

Best Forgotten

Who are these people putting heads on chopping blocs
without a care for their dear lives
are they the martyrs or revolutionaries
or another bands of renegades
some skinned to reveal flesh
others hung by nearest trees
then the ones exiled to dark waters
in cells where a sun ray struggles
to breakthrough
of times when the art of revolutions
was a genuine desire
freedom to breathe in fresh air
without the stifled inhale
holding close to arms and chests
torchbearers in elongated shadows
spring a surprise out of the hat
chasing away the brigands who never could be won
in day of tryst of destinies
when the cymbals began to thump
no one among the revelers
knew the art of revolution's

Amock on Run

I knew a river
cool, clean, clear, crystal
majestic flow from the heights
it rushed through
valleys, gorges, plains
bringing along
songs of harvest
ripe yellow fields of mustards and
sun flowers too
till a civilization knew of its birth
it flowed relentless
some tales within its fold
belonging to the gods
a cradle of humanity on its banks
the pious river takes along the sins of washed souls
it was a few decades ago
now a mudded, puddle in splash
industrial spills, the gospel of a polluted spring

Blue Count

Blue the color of royal blood
Skies shine sparkle blue
Vastness of oceans glued in blue
Apples of eyes are blue eyed boys
Blistering beauty of blue eyes
Fortune of gold heaps for blue eyed wanderer
Blue a color of life
A life giver
Making breathing possible
Of all the luminious
Its blue which only counts

Prophecie Riddle

Let me live in my dreams
Be it nightmares
A ride on white elephant brings luck beyond compare
If it were to be seen in wee hours
The dream run would continue
Of fads and imaginations
Old grand mum's advise
Shrill whistle during night
Leading to state of penury
And bankruptcy written in gold bold
The same goes for thumping of
wooden desks
Not to be left behind the pundits join the melee
Conjuring of stars and whirlwind motion of planets
Determine the fate lines
The fault lines to be corrected
By ornamenting fingers with
Precious stones to woo the lady luck
For the will full and practical
A pack of sheer nonsense to be discarded
As the fate rolls into slumber
Efforts bring disaster
Omens, soothsayers, glib tongued, oily orators
Feed on weak, wilting, weathering,

Stone Hearts

A time to tell a tale of love
Screams, blood letting,and bombings
A time to drown in those wishful moments
Books abound in wars and battles
Teaching the craft of math to confound
Or lapping it up with slices of scientific wisdom
To invent a disaster
Humans driven by desires
Only the feeble indulge in game of hearts
Belittle a emotion called love
It's a pity to fall for it
Sucked in by pretensions
Stone the Romeo
Hang the nomad of far east by nearest trunk
Grave in the Arabian love fanatic a lunatic
A time to tell tales
When love meant life
Passions gifted from heavens
A frown on face to speak of
Meant stealing of breath

Treasure Hunters

A Mount of snow filled jar
A view from the window
To much lapped in by laps of nature
Sun rays reflect brilliant from the glue struck ice
Snowy abound swell in swollen winters
In swelter of summers
A cool dash of swift current
Only the dweller knows
A jewel thrown in dust
Nomads of treasures hunters
Fake in jetty bound journey
Dwellers in bounties
Reap in fortunes
Of less material
Pure clean nectar swifts
Brooks of honeyed springs
Greens the signs of reckoning
In polluted lands the treasure hunters
Finds long lost legacies saddled
In fortunes gutted, jettisoned, for lures luring

Devil's Chirp

Eyes elusive in search of polished souls
Cracked pieces of heart in disarray
Some deep in disgust, others contemplating a disaster
Royal robes draped in daggers long and skimmed
A polished soul, in a heart cry
Found one languishing high and dry
A textbook saint
Or a bearded statue looks like roots of tree climbing to infinity
An axe to grind
Polished masses devoured, consumed, catapulted
To heights of glory
In a saints wedding the devils sing a folklore
Polished souls deep in echoes long and lost

Ultimate Survivor

Silent cascades from eyes
Tell a fable of humanity submerged
When the palm lines crossed at impromptu
Not even the bow at the altars saved the day
As the still waters hold the depths
Salty, tasteless, stinky, tell tales timely
Knew of a beggar duped of nears and dears
For him the time moves as a raft sinks towards the abyss
They robbed everything he had
His palms were empty vassals
A few of them surviving on his forehead had an indifference
Take the fortunes
Muck up the inhale if any
Survival instincts hold up the barrage
Where love deserts
Men all foreign vanish as shooting stars
A few lines for a survival
An antidote for the sting thousand a times

Return of the Prodigal

An elder held the storm by a whisker
He could turn a mole hill into a mountain
Or a torn rag into a flying carpet
The discarded broom into a magic wand
Well over a century,he had his jaws as firm as a granite
Not a single strand lost or on the grey side
By a move of the wind the rainfall came at the snap of his fingers
No one knew who he was,where he came from
No friends,either foes
Neither riches nor the fortunes
The village by the side of flowing sounds flourished
His hand soothed, his touch calmed
Then one day he vanished
No one heard of him ever again
In some other place,a being over a century
Rolls laughter into houses unknown, homes broken

When time passed by a flick of clock hand
The motion censuring the limit to be reached
One odd oddity oblique
Challenging the might of right
Grow beyond your shadow
Leap above the boundaries set
Defy the wretched destiny
Make hay while it shines

With a pluck of dirt count the carrots
A brain to hold the heist
A fistful of dollars to seize
Old haunted houses where the backyards had buried gold baked brics
Diving in depth unrevealed
To fish out the fishy treasures
Belonging to a pirate lord
Ambits overgrown beyond ambitions
Humans portray a caricature
Of a future well in sight
But certainly out of reach

Love Royal

Palace in a land of warriors
Where royalty oozed
In moonlit nights the love lorn lovers languish
A loyal love for the royal regal
Time almost stilled when two hearts met with one song
Only the cursed fate knew the destinations
Away from the land of seven seas a princess
The royal touch becomes a flamed passions
In silent sobs the loyal love sings a solitary dirge
In moonlit nights passions flicker
The royal now a minced lover thorned by two roses
Call of the duty, a battle to be won or a life to be given
A tearful farewell by the loyal,a warm hug by the loyal
Swords cut the effigies to bits
A sly, spear, slices
In a funeral procession the loyal kisses the flames to be immersed in immortality
The royal in trance watches the high rise flames from the heights of the palace
To be immersed in a wallow of pity

Brown Death

Smoking Joe, he wore a hat to cover his bald plate
Cool, calm, collective in disposition
Once he flew of the handle no one ever knew what would happen
A pint of spirits and some pork to keep up the cheer
Poker up his sleeve, he always won in a gamble
Joe a gentle giant
A total family man to the hilt
Many would say chip of the old bloc
He carried the burden without a sigh
Up front barging through the dark clouds
Somewhere he knew the cruel stars had played a trick
Never to hide a tear or miss a hearty laugh
Joe the spirited one kept the dark secrets away
Phantom cells took their toll
His eyes encircled death
Never to sigh
His spirits gave in to the monster
Smoking joe never smoked again
A cigar of a monument
Chocolate in taste, the brown death entices

Sage Curse

In sea of wonders
Blue waves where the fish kingdom survived
Millions of them swap in jelly battle
For a dart of food the jostle begins
Sages command they belonged to the lords above
Somewhere in the mid of blue paradise a serpent twice the size crawled
The legends said the lord had send his heir
As the sun started sunning sultry
The lake of lords became a stinking mess
Millions of bones laid strewn in the graveyard
No one saw the crawling heir
They all perished in front of the fireball
The face of evil in skin burning heat
Lands of harvest erupt in bonfires
A body stripped of flesh
The bones support the rickety framework
Let alone a grub, even a drop comes as a curse

A Drop for Throat

All of them didn't scramble for copper
They never digged deep diamonds
Hoardes marched in for water
Ponds, lakes, and the glacial dwells shrink into puddles
Who ever thought a glass would be priced as a nectar drink
Somewhere in the glassed chamber
A stock from different heaven
Play, splash, dash around in gaiety
Bullions stocked in iron rods
A diamond necklace looked never so bright
Spades and sickles never undone
Mount in treasures sojourn
High rise place, high and dry
Wrath of gods, or a curse from the angels
Nobody's creation, it just rolled out like a Infant from a lap
Now a uncared, vagabond, let loose

Morsel for Living

It took ages for the cymbal beats to reveberate
Rejoicings recur at the reap harvests
Wheat granaries as a wish fulfilled
Eyes look on somewhere in folds dried
Never was a mother so inconsiderate
Heapings on bent backs over the ploughs
For a few stalks of wheat
Bountiful of star specked pearls were exchanged

Indifferent Virtue

Invaders in full cry
Looters of a ravaged civilization
Pooping way the glorious glories
Fragments in reminiscent bygones
Smouldering stacks, a few burning logs, a haze of burn fire mist
No body survived the bloody vampire dance
In a sea of bloodletting
From among the brandishes
A soldier somewhat of lesser legacies
Carries a wooden framework of walnut dried
With a testament in his backpack
They looted the gold wares
I was cotend to save a sacred text
From the bonfires of hell soldiers under devils command

Dark Epics

A discovery of the time unfurl
An age when the celestials ruled the spheres
They speared with the demons for the nectar
Sages commanded when they cursed
Followed by the truth one
Word from an elder meant life or death
For a vow even a kingdom was bartered
Now the dark epic begins
Perhaps the lengthiest one
It goes with a hinder
Wealth commands the efforts
Lost in a wreath of a garland
A pigmented rose, scarred face of a sphere
Lost in furls of slipped eras

Serom of Anthill Antic

Looked, searched, hymn day and night
In a small place called a heart
Finally glimpsed at the wonder
No one ever saw what a heaven looked like
What the forbearences of hell were
Across the streaming sands
Or through the snowy bounds
A heart knew where it transversed
Musings of the passed counsel
Meant all Greek to a jostled soul
Waters of ice cool wastes
Failed in their submission
In a dry spell of heartless sermons
In a place dear he found the answers
A journey so dear wasted
Shade of umbrella in a fiery moon sprinkles
Even the spikes of thorny sun
Did not Pierce the epidermis

Skin deep pleasures, awesome sights of stone gravelled figurine's
Swayed by the senseless senses
Mind commits an omission of sins
Sages as hard as rocks, hermits dulled by mediation
Years of penance laid waste by a flash of a second
Ordinary mortals with wayside morals

Where the gods faltered, the born under the sun waylaid by the acts of sin
One commandment for stoning to last drop
Other wills for sterner acts
An emotion for nothing
A boundless journey with no ends
Hard companions with turtle shells
Sting the life away, the stelled cage of howler
Keeps the destined ones way to far

Fire Ball Explosions

Whose effigies burn
In the mist of smoke twigs
Amid fireball explosions a trio of effigies leap up in sky high sparks
Evil beyond evil confined to the fires
Somewhat of a different kind
An effigy lits up in the shine of the morning shine
It belonged to the beleaguered mankind
Scream, shrieks, a pale of a resemblance of past
In the last throes of drown
It stretches to the saviour's
Hands which feed the seeds of existence
Now content with honey laced poison
An effigy a picture of extreme towed dilemma
Even the time failed to know its ultimate demise

Brail of Heart

Not even the slightest of the birds twirl of the feathers
Insane suffocated, humid in and out
Tales of home spun remedies
A smattering of connotations of love whispers in dying throes of a fatal clasp
Fainting beats succeeded by a not so aweful a pulse
Tremor of divulge cascades
Roar of a hungry loin trapped inside a sparrows heart
Voluminous in length and tragic in breath
Some hidden in the landscapes of time, others vault into open spaces
Mercy non existent, extreme drags for sure
Into a fire ocean, a fire scattering river
A leap beyond the ordinary
Bystanders wrote a standing ovation

Pine Cottage

Lonely house among the woods
A decade of life in climes of sublimes
Away from home in a still frame
Poverty striken land lords with larger than life gifts
Merciful in appearance and more so in disposition
A Weaver working all time around the housemistress with her rounds
To them comes happiness from chores of bread and butter
Even an iota of compassion of others would be a gesture beyond the ordinary
Fate plays its tricks with wicked slips
Curse of cruel time
On a cot the mistress coughs away in violent stream of puff and huff
Even deeds of kind heard fall deaf ears in the eyes of majesty
She gives in to vexed curse
A stoic weaver leaves aside the rituals to put the wheel of life into him
Mistress gone long and back
Weaver still goes with his machine through the night
House in lonely woods does a word of good.

A Ride to Hell

Hells in abound without any bounds
From beneath the grounds to be found
Devils astride the hounds lounge in rest places of death
Sounds of claw without a flaw
Paws as a saw come as claws without any flaws
Grip tightens to sip any clips of venemous blood
Fountains of zips oozes from the rips
Lips on roll to do a remarkable dole for any soul
When the ale without a bail
Reasons fail and hells messengers hail
In arms of the jail without a bail
Pale as graveyard to rail the secrets of sail
Vales to be conquered by the tails
Frills of baked passion served on grills of drilled sullied, buried, exhales in Qualls
Bin of loads with some din
Without any fins just for sins
Kins with the alms
No balms Without any calms
Palms of sin with usual qualms
Those in claim never to blame
Hate flame ever so lame to claim
Bait to overpower the gait
Hate Without any rate Slated to be slained or craned in caged of drained
Feigned upon slained upon pests of detests at best in rest

Parasite of Blues

Yeasts of burden of ages better without the zest.
Race to be hurled in stones without any atone
Braces without any faces
In hinds without any wind
Tone of a zone in distress
No bind to find
Sinner the winner, hand in assaults to insult
Arms of the loved by beloved
Bleed in currents of torrents
Contrived, deprived, without a hint of dint
Lots of sorts mount to count the sermons in exile.

Wind Stealer

It never galloped nor did it glide
Those who saw the diamond said there was never like him
He whispered to the clouds, he could surpass the wind knot
Robin of the forests, the fame proved a curse
Doomed by a doomsday resurrection
His legs started shattering, even a limp seemed a far away
The feudal lord looked at his Odyssey
You shall be rested in the way you deserve
Ear rings of gold, a white coffin for the last rites
The bullet which hit the race lord knew its mark

Milk Robbers

They milk me no end, and still some worship
When the sun sets, they come in hush to take me away
Udder lovers, the milk robbers
After pouring the last drops out
I am pushed, shooed, and an unwanted ornament on the roads
I am called the gods by whom I know
Acquaintances of golden legacies, men from the heavens descendant

Dreams on A Wheelchair

My rosy apple as fresh as green from the yards
A smile to disarm the mightiest of the devils
There was non like her
A cruel stroke of fate had something else scripted
Her gazel eyes rolled in convulsion, her gait ricketted
In a wheelchair the gods of earth watched the spectacle
From pity to sympathy, even the bells failed to ring
In a wheelchair the bag of misfortune travelled
Hopes like pearls in a smoke filled sea
Even the misfortunes giggle at times
They tow the wheelchair from one end to other

Rest Incline

Last Ray of the setting sun
I have seen it all
The heartbreaks, backstabs, or even a heartburn
Elements were kind, seasons beautiful
Birds brought cheer, the breeze always by the side
Friends far and few, no shortages of foes
They taught surprise, shock and awe
Regrets and remorses banished
Last Ray of the setting sun rises to see an array of expectations
An analogy to life
Hope in the dancing storms,a gasp in singing tempest
Over and over, time and time
Over the fading tree line, in a silvery mist
To a final retreat
The last Ray of the setting sun

Solitary Vagabond

A bloc head on road
Where the mind is shut free
Wordly worries, or wordly wisdom
All thrown to winds, all washed by the shore
By all counts a worthless bloc head down the road taught a lesson or two
Where diseases come as a beehive of bees
Not a fret, nor a worry, never in a hurry
Singing along the road, the tramp
A thing for all seasons, the bloc head on the road teaches
Fortunes on dwindle, possessions swindled
Never a mind to mind
Living by a thread, in a little comfort, from some galvinized spirits
A mad hatter, strange whacky wierd,
Bloc head on the road trudges merry
Followed by an army of cut throats
Engrossed, engulfed, endangered

Ambulances in Hiding

A last limp
No tall skyscraper, where are the modern gadget's
A cot of death in which a carrion is carried
Sturdy and muscular men of few pounds carry the death stretch
Ambulances in hiding never had the black smered roads to gear one
A somewhat young one, sees the ultimate fate
Carried on the back by a hassled father
A few last drops for the trembling lips
Skyscrapers are far off, ambulances in hiding
The game of rippling I'll fate played till date
A stranger of no consequence runs his hand over the ruffled little ones head
Wish to be a God and grant the boon of livelihood to the young one
The fading pulse, rollicking eyes in search of the envitable
A final smile and the collapse
Skyscrapers are far off ambulances in hiding

Smiling Sun

In a stone inscription, or by the portrait hung on a fading wall
A waxed figure to impell
They the rebels, blew a trumpet
In close heels army of hunger bellied souls
Not of the morsel kind, an urge bigger than the heart larger than the life
Lifeless beings entrapped in fetters, dudgeoned in cudgel's
Smiling sun like a dew drip on a sand blaze
Ultimate of the seasons, a snow blizzard in a autumn spring
High velocity canon balls blew on the faces, the buzz of bullets never ceased
Never short of bold, men of gold
Barren and chilled hard buyonets
Smiling sun the forgotten warriors
Where to hide their rotten, stinking corpses
Anthills of humanity, come in a hail
Looking for their dead heroes
Never again to be found but always heard near and far
A smiling sun, rises in backyard
Impoverished, bony, skeleton child
Perhaps a rebirth or a gift from the Lord's

Dry Honeycomb

Throughout months a silent army is at work
Plucking juices from wild berries, sucking sweet stigmas dry
The honeycomb on the bend branch becomes big and bigger
In wind storms or a rainy lash it stays where it was
Millions of black bees bundle in with dint of fingers
Prying eyes of the silent assassin eye the booty with hunger intent
Scarfed in with thick pads to ward of the poisonous stings
Torches of heat and rising flames, the heist had begun
With hornets nest stirred, little buzz warriors fly off in combat mode to safeguard possessions
Huge licking flames, the last hurrah of the silent army
Masked thugs make off with honey packed in bottles
Dry honey comb a picture of ash on the road
Spooning in the thefts into their overstuffed mouths
A meal of a lifetime on a grave of a dry honeycomb

Vicious Concubines

The unholy scriptures commanded to lead the honey laden trap
Majestic kings, shiny knights, never defeated knights fall like insects in the jaws of a pitcher plant
Bred in poison and bathed in Royal blood
Rewriting pages that never became a part of history
Empires changed on pleasure dice
Armies halted by a signal of a eye lash
Poisonous concubines,a breed bred in poison
Virtually blue all over, even the air exhaled spits the fangs of blue Royal
No dreams, passions burrid in graves
Living on a kill for a moment of lifeless love
The command of blue Royal, determines a fate unwritten, unseen, unheard, unfelt

Hills Brown Skies Red

Hills brown skies red
Something gone wrong with the creators mind
Green patches on hills are missing, the blue floating sails in skies are long seen
Bushfires, massacre of pines, willows, or a stem standing
Fashionable walnut cots to decorate the dream houses
Hills stripped, skies ripped
Smoke filled salad houses
Mint green fodder for the giant mansions
Let there be no hold on the charge
Let's spare no effort leave no stone unturned
To make the hills brown skies red
Some four footed mammals and avians of varieties existed a couple of decades ago
Roads stretch into the farthest limits, train tracks zoom into remotest of corners
A flight to the nearest town on a jet in a backyard
No hills in sight just a barren land of zombies
Skies crimson as smoke screened horizons fade in the gloom of a civilized wonder yet seen nor deciphered

Pearls in Peril

A stranger of lands unknown and out of sight
Comes to dear earth
Alien in land of the shining sun and brilliant stars
Stumbles into a over crowded market
The wares for grabs surprised him
In a big arcade a brigand sold the merchandise to teeming Gatecrasher's
The alien all askance and mouth gaped
The catalogue included dishonesty, deceit, deception,
On a somewhat secluded corner a small timer indulged in wares of no ones interest
Truth, integrity, the moral spirit sold for nothing
Alien wondered and collapsed at the ruined spectacle
A land bestowed with all the majestic Sapphire's
Neither the freeze cold, nor the melt temperature
A hell hole of a existence
Souls selling salutations
Fickle headed demons living in a trapped bait
Aliens opens his wings as huge as the span of clouds
Of and away to land of cool climes
Where sun failed to touch the frozen pastures
Storms hardly made a whisper
Seas never existed and disturbed
Tremours forsaken in a land where the alien arrived form

Gramaphone Crackle

A horror of a wedding night
When the crafts came crashing
Idiot boxes were non existent by then
A huge transistor now somewhere in the dark attic
A testimony to the broken thread
The groom scamped of to frontier
A last kiss planted said a different story
Moist eyes, no tears, just dry pitiless emotions
Phenomena of black death raged to a feverish limit
Men killed men, humanity blooded by humanity, brother speared a brother
The crafts bombed the last of the erect things in a sea of rubble and smolder
Tiny tots of a park buried in grave
The crackle of the huge gramaphone stilled the blood in frozen disbelief
Private Rony no more
Time shadowed by a dark cloak
Life goes on despite the lengthiness of a nightmare
Last kiss planted had a different story

Sirens of Grave Bells

Words forgotten
Have I made a error, or have I missed remembering
Words couthed in a mystery
The mind shuts of the miseries
The being lets loose the devils intentions
No matter the time which defaults
Betraying at a time when most wanted
Words of wisdom or a sheer piece of nonsense
Forgotten and confined to cowb ridden monasteries
A time a pulse of a stealed moment when the ox ridden demon called for the head
In times of convulsions, a breed of persons rejoicing in pleasures of seconds
Rotten, repulsive of a degraded bunch
Eating from the hands of a mortality long lost and probably forgotten
Idols of a fragments dumped in chests of long lost lumped lampoons
Who remembers, regrets, repents, those unforgivable souls if ever to stay in the memories of those tiny tinges in a bedridden chamber

Hunting Love Doves

I knew the stab
True lies, a love hardly flowered
Spring medows in hush tone falls
Rise and fall, ebb and tide
Angry outburst, a dew cool whiff
On a summer day in a blister hot air blast
A air blew to condense the drops in a freeze
Power hoofs of cannines drive a sledge through a glacial dwell
Two souls ripped in blood and heart
Hate mongers, love slayers, wild guns, ugly jaws, and even more uglier minds
Cannines the messengers of hope in wilderness
Bullets shred the breed apart
Another fairy tale and a ghostly end
Who knew to love, gave up a life to people of tight fisted quorum

Farewell to Pride

Heartless existence
A body within a soul
Almost lifeless, to the limit vacuum
Rage of raging bull, horning a still statue
Indifference of a variety, turning backs on heroes farewell
They watched with a cruel glint, spat with infinite contempt
Guns of freedom, for whom no eye shed a tear
Ages gone into ages
Often a repeated grotesque
No respect for foes who foiled
Ridiculed and almost hammered into a sheet
What's left of a pride
Merely a stack of bones, covered with stink flesh
Carriage ridden men with horse straps of golden thread's
Dab on mouths with perfumed silken scarf
As a freedom gun lay with a body stripped of a soul

Heart and Head

Wearing a heart on sleeve
In vain they all drain
Think with a head or heart
Wise council, advised put your rocker straight
Learn the art, don't be a dart
Weakling, a streamless path
Only the heart followed, head swallowed
Marooned and shipwrecked
Tossed about with gay abandon
Head a machine of tricks
Heart ever so and full of flicks
A total loss declared a council
A good for nothing shouted another one
Only the heart beats along with the tiresome
A treacherous journey smoothed by a song

A Celestial Affair

Child's eclipse
Moon o dear moon
A face of a father or mother
Long time lost in wild fire gunfire
A child of lesser god, watches with a innocent horror
No place for cries, tough tramp cracks the survival nut
Living on what may seem a frugal existence
In those deary moments
When the world's gone to sleep
The face of a moon
Shining like Sapphire in skies
Face of a father or mother
Cool rays radiate radiant
A urchin, an unwanted, a uncared
The wretched gunslingers took away his life
Always in that moon sprinkeld fountain
A child of lesser god watches the moon face

Life in Capsule

If you can't be anything be something
If you can't hate spread peace
If you can't love set a few pigeons free
Can't be a traitor be a patriot
Can't blaze like a sun twinkle like a star
Can't flow like a raging ocean be a gurgling Brook
If you fail to compete learn to try
Can't be a loin be a tiger
Can't be a heart stealer be a giver
Can't be knight of dreams, be a fearsome horsemen
Can't be a sinner be a sage
Can't be a winner, be a game loser
Can't be a cheat, be a swindler
Can't be a huge rock, be a giant pebble
Can't be famous be infamous
Can't be a sorry sight, have the courage to wipe a drop
Can't be a man be a child with an innocent heart

Hate of Religions

A time for red sun
Dark, grey, cloud gathering night
A distant way, thousands of murdering jackals
Armed to teeth, soaked in hate, bathed in contempt, washed with sin ontiments
Not scared, not afraid, for death awaits the time ridden future
Some brothers, from among the marauders
The jackals are scavenging, razing love built homes
A few guilds for a new dawn
Toddlers and a frail looking thing
The jackals descend down like hungry blood seeking vampires
Fugitives of native land
Bushed, bugged, gaged,
Reach for the trolley ride over the river
Brandishing the metals the jackals race down to stop the fleeting trolley
The fleeing household reach their elk
Head buried in hands
He watches the smoke of his house erupt in flames
When humanity was altered for sake of a religion
A tale told by an elder during the partition times when the state of Jammu and Kashmir in northern part of India was torn apart by religious strife and humanity all but forgotten in the wake of attainment of freedom from the British.

Sea Exodus

A sea gull and a cup of woes
Was a time when a full flew with the waves
High rise the gigantic one was on the top of charts
Clear reflections of the beam and the dive proved early bird catches a fish
Huge huge and pretty huge the expanses pleased the gull
Living to tell a dream come true was what the bird imagined
Then out of the corner a black monster appeared on the high seas
Perhaps an iceberg had changed colour
It moved through the gushing waters
Tearing the heart out of the pleasing ocean
Disturbed, the flight of gulls thought of an immediate invasion
Fish for catch became thin
The water to drink a bit too thick
In a sea storm the monster disappeared under the waves
The water became black slush
Trouts floated on the water surface as corpses laced by an invader on a plunder city
A gull takes a flight from the surrounding madness
Driven out from the inhabitation
An exodus from the sea lands
To be seen and heard

Missing Chirps

Its five in morning
Usually got tuned to a few chirps of the white dove pecking at the window
A view of the green rocky sprawl through the open window
Cool monsoon showers overcoming the heat and sweat
Sometimes the flash of thunder light through the slit
Stirred and stir
In a old granny's house where once stood a village
No concrete blocks of iron or huge cement ricks
Pillars of oak supported the mud thatching
It was a wonder
Airy, wavy, salubrious
Slept like a log throughout the day in summer breaks
A change of routine dulled to perfection
Artificial air to creep into bones to give limbs a shaking
Wretched little monsters to bite and sting and keep up awake
A use or abuse of science
When it snaps the tantrums come free
Insomnia is what the medicals term it
Its five in the morning
Eyes sore with unrest
Face puffed with contort
Perhaps a tweet of a sparrow to raise the sleepy stocks

The Greatest

A crank in ring
Hailed as a bull fighter
He swayed like a butterfly, stung like a bee
A full blow could vaporize
Opponents feared him, the crowds went delirious as he danced in the ring
The greatest was truly the greatest
Fame, fortunes, and fads
He grabbed them all
Somewhere the angel had a different story planted
Pounding on the head, created a downs syndrome
He who knocked down with a single hand could barely eat with two
His head shaked like a new born
He could progress a few yards with supports
Somewhere the angel had a different story for the greatest

If Only

If only a life could be lived again
If only a few individuals met again
If only a dream came true
If only someone walked and stayed
If only a time arrived
If only childhood rearrived
If only school days came forth
If only those pranks were enacted
If only the parrots came on the windows instead of alarm clocks
If only the Brook by the side of the cottage house flowed brilliant blue
If only a picture on the wall talked
If only a prince left his possessions
If only someone was crucified
If only the fields reaped green harvests
If only nature stayed the way it was
If only a war would not come
If only a despot would be in midst
If only the race for treasures ended
If only brotherhood rained
If only humanity reigned
If only guns were roses
If only gun trotting soldiers were innocent children
If only fallow lands were apple orchards
If only sand dunes were a queue of tulips

Cruel Misgivings

No place for a heart to reside
Truly vast universe of unseen celestials
Grand dame civilization sunk in sands of time
From the time when scripts came to vogue
Countless came to be devoured only the heart where to reside
Mellowed in dire consequences
Enmeshed in faceless controversies
Only when the brain followed the heart
Swept away by tide epidemics
No cures in charmers pouch
When destruction occurred, desolation stared, black death stalked the white land
A piped charmer blew in notes
A heart knew of a place to reside
Reduced to bony skeleton
Punished in heaven made to starve in hell
A heart knew of a place
Coaxed to sing in fire springs
Made to hunt in despair
In dim lit chambers of a devils paradise
An angel amid a night mare

Echoes of heart everywhere
Strife unbearable
Thrive in thinkable

Echoes of heart in distance
They fill in with soft, cushioned, pies
Contort when hot gales blew on faces
Dear not so dear everyone
Echoes of heart, sublime in touch, sombre in dispositions
Deserters in dozens, unfaithfuls in scores
In those giggle laughters a tale of deprive hidden like a scythe
Scoundrels borne off concubines womb, bimbo of harlot's desire
A contempt up brought in villainous lullaby
Time to recollect echoes of heart
Spurious creatures decked in hyenas skin
Sly as jackals scowl, a wolfish creature
Drowned in pools of mystic spirits of buds from poison paradise
Rested in palms of echoes of heart, ensconced from the titillating ventures of a delved mind

Innocents Desire

I know when the heart skips a beat
When a tear drop rolls of from the chubby cheeks
Little one off balanced and takes a tumble
When the tantrums take them to bed without a food
When the teeth start rolling out giving the impression of a toothless tiger
When the fever touches a new limit and face is all flushed red hot
Throws arms and legs in despair on not going to school
Closes nostrils to gulp in milk, makes faces on getting veggies to eat
When the tiny one disappears in mid of night, to master a fall
When the needle pierces the soft skin for a dose
Heart skips a beat when its all lonely
In confines of four walls without the giggles and laughter

Ever in Long

Drop of tear from eyes of a heart
Long passed into history, in a confine of a page
When knights wrestled for a heart
Kings threw thrones to rubbish for a heart
World was forsaken for a place in heart
Love touched summits, fired ordinary mortals into legendary heroes
Time when the heart shed a tear from its eyes
Long lost in sands of time
Imprints washed by the time clock
Now a gamble, only played by the tricksters
Wonder where is the passion lost
Gone in winds, lost in madding crowds
Webbed in hate filled Minds
Love in trickles in rivers of tight fisted sprouts

Soft Ailings

Its time you reached me
Time as old as the hills beyond reach
Earthy pond holds the depths of sublimity
Pure as the blood in blue veins
Its time you reached out to me
Baked in sweltering sun, some fragments excavated from a city of broken hearts, a topsy turvy Riddle
No one knew the answers, on a splash wave of speculations a sand house of dreams came alive
Its time you reached out to me
Time enveloped in folds of dark satin sheets
A bubble of dreams lost in graves of wild mulberries
Its time you reached out to me

Reckoned Hour

Hour that never came
Warmth in air, coolness around
A happy ending to a fairy tale
Prince on red stallion, holding spear
A hour that never came
No one whip, looking for the one who could swipe
Done to perfection, disgraceful acts,
Somewhere in simmering depths of a scorching lava
A heart that only knew to beat for a name plunges in last rites
A hour that never really came
A flowering bud and a rose Lilly garden
Merchants of fate, desperados of enclosed hate
Stifling grip of mongers
Robbed them of a pleasant journey
Hour of peace never came
Crowds of disposed humans
Lost in mindless accumulations
A dream that actually could have happened

Soft Ailings

Its time you reached me
Time as old as the hills beyond reach
Earthy pond holds the depths of sublimity
Pure as the blood in blue veins
Its time you reached out to me
Baked in sweltering sun, some fragments excavated from a city of broken hearts, a topsy turvy Riddle
No one knew the answers, on a splash wave of speculations a sand house of dreams came alive
Its time you reached out to me
Time enveloped in folds of dark satin sheets
A bubble of dreams lost in graves of wild mulberries
Its time you reached out to me

Hour that never came
Warmth in air, coolness around
A happy ending to a fairy tale
Prince on red stallion, holding spear
A hour that never came
No one whiped, looking for the one who could swipe
Done to perfection, disgraceful acts,
Somewhere in simmering depths of a scorching lava
A heart that only knew to beat for a name plunges in last rites
A hour that never really came
A flowering bud and a rose Lilly garden

Merchants of fate, desperados of enclosed hate
Stifling grip of mongers
Robbed them of a pleasant journey
Hour of peace never came
Crowds of disposed humans
Lost in mindless accumulations
A dream that actually could have happened
The hour never really happened

Almighty Face

A face of God
Among those smiles
In a faceless mob
Driven by wild fury passion
I saw a face of God
A shriek nightmare, where the hunts screeched into ears, buried into eyes
Souls decapitated, humans coming out of million burrows
A face of God in a faceless humanity
Brighter than morning sun, warmer than a fire glow in winter
Takes heavy loads of despondency away from the back
A cherry smile to set the day on
It held back everything
From nuisances to disappoint
From mock excuses to blundering failures
It binds, makes you surrender the kind
Who is that face among the faceless
A child of weak limbs, fresh red flesh
Eyes deep in sleep, a wild cry to set hearts in motion
When the dear turned away, it gave the pillar to stand apart
A face of God comes once in a lifetime!

Birds on Run

Jittery limbs, rickety gait, had a ever lasting pomp in eyes
Warrior of thousand battles will visit the old crumbling walls
They the wretched pair, from the mystery cottage waited till the last stroke of the beat
They are little, drank a few drops
Folks evesdrop to see them alive or dead
They lived on and on, well into the century
They waited on and on for the warrior of thousand battles
Some act of providence, or a mere coincidence
The long lost warrior appeared in dreams of silenced, dried, misty, suffocated cries
The cottage by the side of the wooded thickets
Bursted with overpowering explosive thunderstorms
The couple of fortitude had the last dream well in eyes

Street Urchin

A Santa Claus for a rag picker
He the one who stroll
In filth, squalor, dirt
Looks for a Santa Claus
Heard in books, seen in fairy tales
Perhaps for a glitter among the heap accumulated by the deserved
Precious gift thrown in haste thinking it of as a waste
Rag picker and his Santa Claus never met
In wildest of dreams
Once that attractive figure
Throwing chocolates, and the treasure boxes at the army of innocents
Who but the rag picker, a specimen of dishevelled human race
Despised, kept away, trodden by all and sundry
A day, in a moment of idleness, I will meet him on the way
Where paths are stringed into a highways
No rich, no poor, just the people with heart count

Midas Touch

My dreams alone haunt me
Looking for the Midas touch
The hand that turns gold to dust
A magic wand to turn grey skies to sprouting rainbows
My dreams alone haunt me
Out from the corner in a siesta
Or a faint flash from far flight
First strike of dawn, or last rites of the dusk
My dreams alone haunt me

Dedicated to Indian sports contingent at Rio for putting in the best and sports lovers throughout the country for never losing hope

Mummy Kings

Roll me like a Egyptian mummy
The Pharoes of the Sandy lands
For a spot in history
In embalmed fine cotton silk
Scents out of crushed roses and stalks of evergreen bougainvillea
The kings and their fantasies
Buried deep in dune monasteries
Now the mundane, of ordinary stock
Look for a spot in history
Wrap up the mummies, in those dummies
Golden coffins, diamond studded nails
Go deep into the brown cover
Similar for a spot in history
Time when the ordinary became kings of alien lands
Pharoes descend on earth
Mummies far and near perhaps everywhere
Just for a line in the chronicles

Scornful Hate

First shunned now embraced
They dug in deep graves to bury me deep
Even when I did not utter a first cry they silenced me
Humans, the barbarians Inflicted with a curse
Never saw the soft side of a new born
Thought off as an unbearable burden, a kind of a donkey load
As I wake up, the cheers on faces of countless
Yet to come off age
I beg in a sojourn of a journey
Throwing the traditional muck at scornful faces who mourned instead of rejoicing
An Everest to be climbed, I look at the sky which is not the limit
The ones who shunned now embrace me

Ill Reputed

Troubled terrian terrier
It was from the shepherds heards
Young bunny grew in cosy comforts
Nothing of the wild variety
Quality food instead of mashed corn flower cakes in sour milk
The troubled terrian terrier survived the ordeal
Then all of a sudden its paws starting inching giant size
Jaws opened wide to reveal set of sharp pincers
It gained bull strength, broke open fritters, chased trespassers full in flight
Trouble terrian terrier became a nightmare
It jumped from heights to scare the daylights out of unaware visitors
It humbled in every way, carrying bum bitten strangers for the needle dips
A lurking danger snapped in, it took the crawling thing in its fearsome jaws
Ripped open the poisonous viper
Trouble terrian terrier lived up to its repute

Pounded and Pillaged

Dragging pounds of fresh cloud cover
A mist envelops the layers of heart hidden hide
Deep down flakes of memory swell to tell
Times come by to shade into fades
A few couplets itched in gravelled granite
When time ticks telling
Two hearts with one song
Centuries lost to cruel clocks
Shine of emperors shunned
Queens well into bygone era's
Stripped of hearth and heaven
A sake of a pity emotion
Wasted in high and dry letting
Long misty silence, silvery overhangs across the love vale
Where one day perhaps two hearts with one song would meet

Don't take the heart which belonged
Kings had those awful riches
Emperors belonged to a high creed
I only had a heart which no longer belongs
Marooned by a bay somewhere on a lonely strip of an island
My only possession, dearest of the dear, a gem among the diamonds
Don't take the heart which belonged

No more wailed longing, the gasping breaths of longevity
Slowly and steady the poison percolated
Ages after ages a tale often repeated
Poor no belong to rich
Wretched faters well below the blooded dignitaries
But the whistle in a heart
Blew the mocked drill apart
A heart no longer belonged
Delving deep mysteries of heart
No one born ever knew
Creator befuddled, his bearers know of none
In those shrilled notes
Of a dead poets imaginative mind
Love the eternal spring of live
Springs forth to burst into life

Creator and his epic
Grew as ordinary seed in a flower bed
Taken by the index finger, thumb sketched in portraits of ancient splashes
Dumped, buried, engraved, a sin of an enslaved soul
Rising like smoke from a ringed hallow mount
Charms of hearts commit the blunders
Waylaid into bone filled chambers
Where the screems burst forth the walls as high as a fort climb
The time it Surrendered to fantasies
Not of a revellers making
Undoing of star stripped sultan
A heart no longer belonged

Hounds of time look for public places to burn live effigies
For felonies which did not have a heart belonged
Rimmed in by the golden cage called honour
Lives massacred, beings slaughtered, with carcasses hung by the ceilings
A fearful reminder by a force of traditionalists
Good to see a bird fluterring with wings clipped
Purists by choice, rejoice shamefully without a hint of woe
All for a pity thing called a heart no longer belonged
Concluded

Lament Chidhood

Cherry faces and their curse
We all chorused it was bright and sunny
Circle around our friends and a mystery handkerchief
Two would be muscular fought over a bone
Wild cheering, claps loud as thunders
School was a mystery about to unfold
Then came those back breaking loads
Laughs into groans and then moans
You need that and you need this
The stick Commanded the flight
Slowly a joy became a burden and then a fright
Loads increased and the love of school deceased
A neighbour's son achieved something out of the hat
Emulate if you can't then the deteriorate
It summed up existence
Child of seven and not that even
Wise men with
Be this, be that
A child of seven and not to even
Thronged the green fields with his prongs
It will kill and probably still
Some nerve which you have
Children are like soft clay dug fresh and moulded into desired shapes by the elders

Black Landfills

Lake, Pond, or Puddle
Times immemorial, blue water creamed against banks
In vision the bubble underneath danced in delight
Almost like star filled sky
Colour of mermaids flashed in mid of night
Suddenly springed a sprout
Black smoke enveloped, a complete haywire
Horse carriages taken of by automobiles
Spacious places swallowed by lofts
Slowly they made us cough to black death
Times immemorial when blue water creamed against the banks
Freshness the beauty of era well into graves
Air a pure intoxicate
Now in thousands masked inhabitants move with fear choked Minds
Is it my dwell
Or a lake, pond or a puddle

Passion To Chase

What has now become a kingdom
Once of a river we all knew
Flowing down the massive slides
Of a cascade between the steep gorges
What remains of a feast to eyes
Brown sands and sharp pebbles
Who took away the gift bestowed
Slicing through the murky clouds a thunder brought a shower
Muddy rivulet appeared down the slide
Bringing old memories down lane
Demons, monsters, hydra headed cannons dotted the landscape of lands
Stole the crown of blue kingdom's
On a high loft bridge
Plain sand coasts and sun washed stones
Greet the eyes
Centuries ago a stranger watched a gushing current
A battle field sized glacier from where rivers clawed out
Shrunk in size downsized by fire pouring skies
What has become of a planet
A dust ball of smoke, fumes, and blares
In those sacred texts mention of the dreaded black age
Truth followed by rule of pure
Now the dark age to be replaced by a blank verse
Never ending trail of a civilization on fathomless tracks

Humans as plastic aliens
Stenching air and pollutes glore
My page dedicated to elimination of Pedraitic cancer so to make the world a happier place for young children to live.
The day this passion folds the page would come to an automatic end.

Holy Beeline

Goddess sits on snow mount
Calling for a day when she would be flooded
Caravans of revellers on a mountanious highway
Through wooded forests along the coast of a river in anger
Wishes in plenty fulfilled
Some beg health others wish for a fortune
A piligrim moves with snails pace
Feet bare pricked with thorns and blood dripping
Starved and thirsted to near death
No one knew the wish
All of them looked askance
With a hymn on lips
Perhaps asking for some strength to move in
She staggered hit a boulder and dropped flat
Then she felt the trunk of a pine and on her feet again
All realised she was blind
Some said she deserves to be at home
Its a foolhardy venture shot a voice
She can slip down a gorge and call it an end
Worshipper quite and sombre
Replied in a certainty
Summit of goddess calls
For on reaching the gates of paradise
I see the world from the shine of her eyes
For me the world comes alive for a fraction
Colour of life the fair of revelers, Mother earth in its sublimity
I no longer yearn for blooded events of current times
For me once in a year the goddess on the summit

Detour in Crisis

A few words, a few lines, a parting gift
Never asked for a long journey
A short detour will suffice
Never ever asked for a smile
Never ever told to wait for me
A heart takes a thump
Misses a secret
Lost in dust of the fading hour
A few words, a few lines
Never of love nor of hate
It took whale of a time
A sin called confession, a felony called indulgence
Never in depths nor in shallow
Will ask for a smile or take a love

Voiceless soul drenched in hollowness
Makes compromises at the flutter of a breeze
Signs in to the utter extremes
Never bears the bric bats in ample
Soul in self, a voiceless inhuman
Drowned in miseries of fatal vices
Submerged in depths of craving desires
No way to trudge a different path
It looks to go on forever
A blindfold army led to a battlefield
A ambition to rattle ages old penance

Not even a hint of put up mercy
In a chatter of cacophony
Voices of souls lost in crescendo of times
Without a rest it looks to prod on

Wafts of Flutter

A time for a flutter of breeze
When it comes
From where it sneek'S in
Hearts on roll, dreams run free
A flutter of breeze is just a wait
Patience of a stone stilled in grave
A centuries old oak stands strong amid a string of broken pines
Cyclones rip through the backyard without a hint of upturn
Storms burst through the city in a ripple
A heart not in distress neither in digressed paths
Looks for a flutter
A poets lonely corner
Or a paupers opera house
Blood stained eye drops in weight of gold
A few taters of parched leaves
Left as priceless possessions
All for a flutter of breeze
Which brings fragrance of roses

Around two decades a roaring blast shook the foundations of my house. Being close to the border it was a time when the Paki arty batteries were pounding the area, nothing unusual about the event. One of my friends came running to inform me that the village grocer had lost two of his sons in the explosion. I just wanted to get into the depth of things and went to the site of the incident. A wall of the house had been flatened due to the blast. On further enquiries it was revealed that the son's had gone to collect led from the bullets buried in sand where a close by army unit practiced firing. Accidentally that had managed to find a old artillery shell. They took the death gift with them. On reaching the house the kids started to price open the shell which exploded on face, killing the boys instantly.

Soon the entire village collected nearby and the wailing started. The mother was in extreme grief. Her cries went around like wild shrieks but to no avail.

Grooms of Dreams

Where will I find them
I see them dressed as grooms, on a robust mare
My toys are gone
I am doomed
Where will I find them
My brides decked in gold embroidered all red
Now I prepare for the last rites
My back gone to pieces
A darkness of a hell paradise awaits me
Where will I find them
If this was a fate was it really
For just a minute let their eyes open
To have a glimpse of the grooms
I have nothing but a empty appetite
My hearts ripped, all lost to cruel time
Where will I find them

A Doodle for My Pot

One thing which carried me was to own a doodle to feed it and savour its delight by choicest of spices. But something else came over to rake in my objectives.
What was it a unbroken bond of unseen love and it unfolded in a dear way

The chick came from the hatch
It seemed quite and ready to go
Cute and very cute
With brown feathers and hare like eyes
Ready to meet the world
Putting the cosy thing in my Palms
With great care and share
It was a guest in my house
Watching it grow in front of eyes
The rooster was all muscles and claws
Upright and bolt straight
I gave it the name doodle
Three months later it gained on
Now the thing was ready for the pots
Got a kitchen knife sharpened
On the day of reckoning it crowned
A stream of unwanted thoughts came over
Feeding to kill, the cruel human streak
As the day held, pity the soul which held
Not any more a doodle for my pots

Let it live in the back yard
It grew for another three months
Walking like a king in the house
Crowing to warm us to the winter sun
Then one day the call stopped
Looking for the places of its errand
A heap of brown feathers and blood clotted
Perhaps gobbled by a jackal
A doodle for my pots holds special in mind

Why does mother earth bleed from the doom Inflicted on it. Rampaging beasts of burden have virtually made it into a hell. Extinction of species is just the tip of the iceberg as more scandles come open to watch the decapitation alive. Dagota protests have caught the imagination of the environmental activists the world over. In arms against rampant commercialisation of a specific oil rich basin these protests now threaten to blow out as authorities are now giving up patience and resorting to force to curb the dissent.

Heist of Centuries

Rag tag bunch in trampoline houses
Almost as a army on a battlefront
Wearing of heat, sunshine, dust
And hunger
They come in all shapes and sizes
From a three year old warrior to a sprightly eighty year
On weekends they pitch in with vigour
Harder the crack of baton the more the resolve
What for you now to drench now
Digged gold, hauled diamonds
Went deep to unfurl ocean pearls
Reached the skies to fill with smoke
Its a brute of a crackdown
Chase the busters to their dens
The inhuman pack, lobosters on a sun dried creek
They survive the assault
A few reminiscent moments
Briused limbs, shattered noses
A limp walk but never in the spirit
Hail humanity of concern

"Kill mills of a creed belong to lower breed
Foul in temper shrieking in growls of blood hunger
Insects on prowl to hide from the brawlers
Burning decks on necks the onlookers heck and peck""

With peals of grudge under a veil
Seal life lines or thousands without heal
For sake of wake all surrender to the bow of the vow
Masses of crass with dim lighted brass to harass
Blooded hands with hooded countenances
Dries the cries of sighes
Masts of pride of in lower casts
Gold platted scripts of reverence in folds of the mould
In bold and cold a tale told to hold
Flawed of debased virtues lamed by weak consciousness tamed by desires and tamed by passions
Scions of demon specters to unleash in high waves the raves to cow and mow
Culled in fires of unholy baptasim dulled by orgy of mythics
Breeded by wash of dulled opium stalks to hack at roots hoot goes into eternity
Of a gale whom all hail
Quail saints on nailed imprints
Ails forever in vales of frosty inhales
Paled into disrepute defaced by the faceless

As per rich hindu philosophy a soldiers death is most respected and one dying on a battlefield is already assumed to have made heavens a destination.
A soldier is lying on a heap of dead bodies but has few breaths to live and does his bit to keep the flicker of life burning.

Tears on Coffin

Boxed in coffin draped in furl
Men of courage to unfurl
Blood in boil, unsoiled love
Words towards sleek in meek masks
In a trick world of the slick
Alone knows the lone voice
On move to prove a truth
Rugs of uniforms of all forms
Riches for the bitches
Stitch of gashes in blistered rashes
In heap of dead when with jackals cry on the hop to feed the remaining cries
A stick to prick the parasites
A few lounges of air for the sacs to keep the fair going.

Earth has been bearing the burden of human sins for many centuries. A creation destroyed to the last by human error than by natures fury. It seeks its revenge on those who tarnished its image.

Contention Bone

Hermits of serenely voices siren in a blare of witchy glare
Gouging out my diamond like eyes stripping my golden tresses
From beneath its sprouts, scooping me all dry
They them all poured poison into my blue sprawl
Snowy abounds without bounds annexed by caravan strings
Rogues to rough up spells of calmness
In vogue to harp at the strings of spun fabric
My times come to gather and snow them with lather
Now prepare for hell in a cell never to be quelled
Anger in swell for species in spiced gels
A feasible way to make life miserable by hand of the invisible
All in arms for mother is a balm
For she will forgive and forget but never regret
Can humanity be in religious books books
On high scale in sacreds a few husts to blow it away in busts
It took few moments for the rooks to be in hooks
Buried in closets zealots pry open clots
Termites in rust ridden dead wood
Gluttons knaw,saw,sivering at the wavering faith loathed

Clothed in doting silken ware,emperors gloating on their creations

Neither opium for an intoxicant nor quixotix potion of concomitants

In brew to sew a dew in springs of autumn, cringes of dot red motifs on blue hues

Grafatti of something, worth of worthless, jewel in lost kings crown, a brown foilet drinking nectar from a jar of adders beehive

Naive pray for grave or crave to pave in wave of time lost raves of stone sculpted walls in emblems of pall

Killing in name of the lords
Banished gatherings in vanished depths
Its a dire something to say of a sire
In fire to tire striken leaper ridden fingers on hire
Sermon chanters for enchants
Rants of crow calls from vaults of mints
Merchants of death called czars now in bazars
Kaiser a miser
Sheets of morgues wrapped in fogs of dirge

CONCLUDED

Epilogue

It has been a refreshing endeavor to write a few lines for my esteemed and respected readers and bring them close to the art of reading poetry which has been losing admirers rapidly. In essence poems capture the voice from the depths of consciousness sought to be put forward by words and using variety of basic poetic devices to give the reader a fair idea of the subject.

A poet would have succeeded in his journey if he conveys his ideas vividly and carves a place of niche among his readers.

The idea of putting random thoughts in form of a complete book had been a long dream since the idea of writing came to mind in 2015. This is work of nine years which has gone into the writing of these poetic collections.

During our school days it may have been the hardy boys or chase novels which kept us busy along with come the soul stirring odes of John Keats or the resplendent descriptions of nature given by bard of Avon, William Shakesphere .Some of the lines are so well written and influence the mind permanently to bring a little poet in hiding from a buried closet.

In times of AI generated literature it is difficult to find thoughts which emerge from originality and strike a chord with readers. The book may not be a perfection of order but one thing which it seeks to promote is keeping the mind where it is and as the prospective reader goes through the book it will be a easy guess to know the true meaning of what is been said in this epilogue.

This book attempts to bring back the love for poetry reading among the die hard fans of the language. Even if a single reader is created I would have succeeded in my effort. The effect of poetry is lasting and can bring qualitative changes in life of an individual. Like all good books which can bring success or failure the same holds for poetry as well.

Last but not the least a word of thanks with all sincerity in heart towards my respected publishers NOTION PUBLISHERS CHENNAI INDIA for making my dream come true. It would not have been possible without their word of encouragement.

Ajit Jamwal
Author
22 February 2024

www.ingramcontent.com/pod-product-compliance
Lightning Source LLC
La Vergne TN
LVHW041146150826
845673LV00001B/77

* 9 7 9 8 8 9 2 7 7 9 9 4 4 *